The Class of
77
Had its Dreams

Gerry Martin

ISBN 9781609201432
Printed in the United States of America
Gerry Martin
All Rights Reserved

Library of Congress Number in process

The Class of 77 Had its Dreams
by Gerry Martin

I would like the book dedicated my
daughters Carrie, Mollie, an Nancy plus Judy

The Class of 77 Had its Dreams

Gerry Martin

TABLE OF CONTENTS

CHAPTER ONE: HISTORY 1

CHAPTER TWO: GEORGE RILEY 5

CHAPTER THREE: COACHES JOHN RICHMOND
AND BUCK ROSE 11

CHAPTER FOUR: BOBBY STONE..............................15

CHAPTER FIVE: JADEN ROSE....................................17

CHAPTER SIX: TIMOTHY CLAUSEN (TIMBO).....................19

CHAPTER SEVEN: DALE RICHTER 23

CHAPTER EIGHT: THOMAS DECKER (THOM)...................27

CHAPTER NINE: GABBY AND JOHN..........................35

CHAPTER TEN: CASEY ADAMS 37

CHAPTER ELEVEN: THE LEADUP 39

CHAPTER TWELVE: THE SEASON 51

CHAPTER THIRTEEN: 25 YEARS FAST FORWARD
TO 2002..93

CHAPTER FOURTEEN: THE REUNION 135

ABOUT THE AUTHOR 141

Gerry Martin

CHAPTER ONE

HISTORY

To steal from the country music group *The Statler Brothers'* song *The Class of '57 had its Dreams,* the Class of '77 of Anytown High School had their dreams. Like any other high school class at graduation, they had endured the joys and tribulations of being students in a school district. Test taking. Time sitting in class listening to the teachers—most of the time. Completing assigned reading and completing assigned homework each day from kindergarten to their senior year. Even so, they spent plenty of time spent having fun at holiday parties, reading books for enjoyment, playground activities, field trips, sharing with friends making new friends and goofing off.

They also spent time at dances, sporting events, shopping, learning to drive, hanging out at fast food locations and just learning to enjoy whatever life threw at them.

Their journey together also had its ups and downs.

Six members of this class attempted to win a State Championship in basketball, along with, of course, teamwork from other class members and underclassmen members.

Their lives before their 1977 school year and those afterward will be covered in these pages. Each gentleman will be generally addressed separately at times and other times with connections to each other.

These young men represented of Anytown High School and community located in southwest Michigan. Anytown is 2 ½ hours from Chicago Illinois, if you follow the seventy-mile-an-hour speed limit.

Possibly two hours if a lead foot is driving.

The six gentlemen's names were as follows: George Riley, Jaden Rose, Thomas Decker, Robert Bobby Stone Timothy (Timbo) Clausen, and Dale Richter.

The Village of Anytown had a population of 2000 people depending on the movement of families in and out of the area at one time or another. The main industry in 1977 was a Hush Puppy shoe factory which employed 200 workers and support staff and a milk processing plant which employed 150 workers and support staff.

The surrounding area consisted of dairy farms and fruit farms. There was a privately-owned grocery/dry goods store and a bank. Three restaurants, one open from 6a.m. to 2p.m., one open from 11a.m. to 9p.m., and the remaining which had a bar within from 10a.m. to 2a.m. There were also two bars in the area which were open from 11a.m. to 2a.m.. One served food with a limited menu and the other had a full menu.

There were two service stations with mechanical service which soon turned into self-service operations for gas and oil and convenience stores. There was a farm supply business, a pharmacy, a post office and a greenhouse. A raceway two miles out of town provided spring and summer entertainment for spectators and drivers both local and far-reaching. There was a convenience store which open in 1979. There was a laundry-mat operated by the owner of the Mobile Home Park and an ice cream shop located in the center of the village.

A hardware store was available for plumbing and building supplies for the weekend handyman.

A car dealership existed in 1977, but three years later it closed up due to lack interest by the owners, who also had an ownership in Nearbytown, seven miles east of Anytown.

Two fruit-processing plants provided a variety of employment throughout the year. There were two grain elevators, one which existed until 1979 until it closed and the other which stayed open a few more years and later developed into a feed mill sales location.

Also in town were an insurance agency and real estate agency. A library was located in the basement of the City Hall. There was a mobile home park with a capacity for 75 units on the north end of town.

A large spring-fed lake was located three miles southwest of the village, called Clear Lake. There was a lesser-sized lake southeast of the Anytown without a public access called Pine Lake and a smaller lake north of the Village called Jenkins Lake.

Property around this third lake had been owned by the Jenkins family since the turn of the 20th Century, and there was a small mobile home park alongside this lake.

The remains of a sawmill also existed at this location. A large number of swine took up residence at this time provided by the Jenkins family.

Those pigs would be a source of discussion in future years.

All the lakes were excellent for the fisherman. An outstanding trout stream existed which meandered through the Village west to east of the north parameters of Anytown. The stream also provided a wonderful day of rowing with a canoe or other floating devices. You could start several miles upstream of the village and float several miles downstream from Anytown. The fisherman, however, claimed the best areas for fishing was just west of Anytown and a couple of miles east of Anytown.

The road that ran through the village was a major highway for travel prior to 1958. Then an expressway was finished which served as the major road.

Family values and faith-based attitudes were strong in 1977. A Catholic Church, a Methodist Church, a Congregational Church, a First Gospel Church and Episcopal Church provided a faith-based structure that benefited large gatherings at each location.

There were two basketball courts in the centrally located park. There was also a tennis court and basketball court behind the middle school and high school. These were readily used by all the youth in the community. Two baseball fields were located a distance away from the elementary school—one for summer activities and one for high school baseball. A softball field was constructed in 1978.

This sets the stage for the early accounts of our six gentleman who are to become the essence of this written word.

Gerry Martin

CHAPTER TWO

GEORGE RILEY

George Riley was the point guard on the 1977 high school basketball team. He led the team in assists and average six points per each game.

Although he didn't have exceptional grades in school, he showed great leadership potential and was a member of the National Honor Society, mostly because of his citizenship qualities.

His dad sold insurance and his mom worked at the cafeteria at the school. He had two siblings younger than he, twin sisters June and Jill.

When George was fifteen until he turned seventeen years old, he helped a friend of his dad, David, run his bread route. He worked on weekends throughout the year. When he reach the age of seventeen, he washed cars for his mother's uncle's dealership in town and helped in other areas where needed.

His great grandmother was born in Dublin, Ireland and came over to America. Her sister Andrea, had settled in New York after meeting her husband Patrick while he was visiting Ireland with his father, who owned a shipping business in America. His great grandfather worked in three different stables owned by city officials. George's great grandmother decided to join her twin sister because her sister was unaccustomed to living in New York.

James and Agnes met at church. Both attended Catholic mass each day. They married and soon afterward moved to the Detroit, Michigan area. James and Agnes' brother-in-law Patrick convinced James that he should assist him in the shipping process across Lake Erie. The couple lived in the Detroit area for two years. James wasn't excited about the shipping business, and brightened up when his neighbor spoke to him about moving to Reese, Michigan, which interested James. The neighbor was thinking of taking up crop farming, namely sugar beet crops. James's neighbor also said it also was a nice area and was more of a rural setting. Some years the crops provide well and others so not much. The family was one of a handful of Irish background families in an area basically inhabited by German ranks.

James and Agnes invited six children into the world. George's grandfather Mike was the second child.

Mike was born in 1910 and married Kathleen McGuire in1938.The depression didn't influence George's kin as much as it did folks in other parts of the country; however, it was still challenge for a family of six children. His marriage to his sweetheart was held off a bit until things picked up a little.

George's dad Daniel was born in1939.

George's grandfather left home for a job 1941, working on erecting power poles. George and Kathleen settled in Jackson, Michigan.

In 1943, George's grandfather fell off a power pole and died a week later from his injuries. Benefits were slim to none for death benefits and such in those days.

George's grandmum never remarried. Daniel and Grandmum Riley were struggling, so Grandmum and Daniel moved back to Reese and worked as a housekeeper for a Catholic priest in that town. They lived in a house owned by the church until Kathleen died of cancer in 1956.

Although George never knew his grandmother, he always spoke of her as Grandmum because that was what he'd called her when he saw her picture on the wall in the family living room when he was learning to speak.

Daniel had just graduated from high school when Kathleen died. Daniel didn't have time for sports, as he had to work a variety of jobs to survive, one of which was sitting and selling his variety of newspapers every Sunday in front of two churches in the area, rain or shine.

After his mother passed Daniel moved to Lansing Michigan to live with his Aunt Mabel. He obtained a job working at an Oldsmobile Plant.

Daniel was a stocky boy at 5'8" and 150 pounds. He liked to go down to the local gym and watch the young men there working on qualifying for the Golden Gloves competition. One day he was asked to be a sparring partner for a gentleman named Don Schmidt, a giant of a man of pure muscle.

Daniel held his own. This impressed the young lady who'd been watching. June Schmidt was in her freshman year at Michigan State University. George had been born in December 1959 and the twins June and Jill two years later. Daniel and June dated, which led to their marriage in 1958. June quit school.

Daniel decided he didn't want to spend all his life in a factory. His wife encouraged his personality for sales so he worked as a car salesman for a dealership in Lansing owned by June's father. He worked there for a little better than two years.

June's uncle, her dad's brother, owned a dealership near Anytown. They thought Daniel would enjoy the small-town atmosphere. Daniel worked there for four years and then decided to sell insurance. He made a good living in this profession.

Daniel was the kind of man who didn't push people to make purchases in whatever sales he was performing. He just stated the facts about whatever he was trying to sell. The client could go from there. Sometimes he'd get riled when pushed by others, but for the most part he was a very gentle man.

Daniel never drank more than one beer and never touched mixed drinks. Some wondered what he'd be like if he did "have a few." They wondered if that calm manner of dealing with life might change.

He occasionally had concerns with how the officials were calling a few basketball games he attended. George's uncle Don had played football at Michigan State University, but although George was a talented athlete, he'd had no offers to continue his efforts at a college or other institutions. However, George continued to play some church league basketball.

He decided to work for his dad in the insurance business.

George had dated Paula Price throughout high school until their senior year. Daniel and June decided that they might be getting too comfortable with each other. George insisted that he and Paula were good Catholic young people, but Daniel and June felt some of the actions they observed in the couple might lead to advancing further. Paula' parents agreed and the couple broke up.

In the autumn of 1976, George fell in love with Mary Klein. Mary's dad, Jim Klein, owned one large apple orchard near Clear Lake and a cherry orchard boarding Clear Lake.

Mary decided to enroll in Western Michigan University to garner a teaching degree. She completed her freshman year and they married in September of 1978.

Jim really liked George, Daniel, and the twins Jill and June. Jim had lost his wife to cancer. She was 53 years old when she died, and they'd been married 30 years. They tried to have children for a number of years. They'd about given up when Mary came along when they were both 38 years of age. Jim was driving a school bus at the time along with his grower duties. Jim really like kids, but the stork never visited again.

Jim never remarried. Mary was years 15 years old when her mother died.

Once in a while, friends would try to set him up. with someone they felt may be a good match. His answer was always similar to a song called *New Patches* sung by a variety of artists. The song says you don't put new patches on old garments, when someone's heart is lying at one's feet, when you've loved someone for a long, long time.

George and Mary built a house on Jim's land a short distance from Jim's house at Clear Lake. Clear Lake was the largest lake in the area, other than Lake Michigan. Like its name, it was full of clear water that sparkled like a giant emerald on a clear sunny day. It was especially beautiful in the spring when the cherry blossoms shadowed on the lake.

George continued to sell insurance and assisted Jim in working on the fruit farm. George played some church league basketball in the winter and league softball in the Summer.

Mary finished her education in 1981. Children had come along—a boy Robert (Bobby) in January of 1980, William (Billy) in March of 1981 and Kathleen came along in July of 1983. Mary substituted as a teacher during the years the children were born and until Kathleen was in kindergarten. She took the children to George's mother June for daycare purposes on those days she worked and earlier when she was attending college.

Mary baked pies and made cider for competitions at various venues. Nine chances out of ten, she'd win the top prize. The truly amazing thing was that she used the fruit not good enough to send to the processers. She'd make applesauce for the family and for the neighbors. The applesauce always seemed to last until the month of March each year.

Jim and George hunted deer in the fall and rabbits in the winter. They were successful enough each year to have venison throughout the months to satisfy everyone in the family.

One such hunt which occurred in1983 stood out from the others. George's dad had never hunted deer before, so George convinced Daniel to join them in the hunt. He wanted Daniel to share in the excitement. He and Jim wanted Daniel to be successful, so Jim spent a few days with Daniel just practicing shooting at a target. Daniel was a quick learner when it came to the skills of the hunt.

On opening day of hunting season, two inches of snow fell. Jim and George had set up blinds from which they could hunt. George had Daniel settle himself in a blind in close proximity to him. Jim went to his favorite spot, where he'd had success for many years. Jim was sitting at the location for an hour thinking about the stars in Daniel's eyes when they arrived at the hunting location. He'd seen this in others' eyes when they'd participated in their first hunts. These individuals, however, were much younger than Daniel now was.

After a half hour, a deer came slowly waltzing by. Jim raised up his bow and shot the arrow at the prey, stopping him in his tracks. Jim slowly approached the huge downed, six-point antlered animal. Jim retrieved George and Daniel to assist in removing the deer after performing the necessary cleaning. Daniel's eyes were as big as saucers all the while.

Two days later, Jim took Daniel with him to his blind. Daniel had shown he was capable of bringing down a deer, so he believed it could happen today. After about an hour, a rather large deer came by.

Jim motioned to Daniel to take aim with his bow. Within a moment, the arrow was on its way. The deer buckled and then righted itself and meandered slowly away.

Jim believed Daniel had made an accurate shot. He told Daniel they should wait about twenty minutes before scouting any blood trail. Jim could see the anticipation in Daniel's eyes. Finally, they proceeded to track the blood, Jim giving instructions along the way.

At times there was a blood trail, and then no trail. Suddenly, the deer was found behind a large log. It was four-point with one prong which had been broken off along its way to his maturity.

Jim guided Daniel in the process of cleaning the deer. Daniel presented his kill to June for her admiration. Both deer were taken to Elmer Johnson, who owned *J and J Grocery* in Anytown. He performed processing on the side in his pole barn, which was a licensed facility.

A week later, June decided join Daniel at the hunting location. Jim had a dentist appointment and George was working at the insurance agency, while Daniel was playing hooky.

After two hours June indicated she needed to pee. When she started to seek out somewhere to relieve herself, she tripped and landed atop Daniel. Daniel's head slammed into the blind and the back of his head was smeared with blood. June propped him up. She asked him if he was all right.

He said he thought he was, but when did she develop a twin?

After June became one person again, she asked Daniel how he was doing. He said he was doing all right. June still had to pee, so she told Daniel to move aside they'd try this again.

*

There's no question that fishing makes lifelong memories for those who enjoy the sport, whether speaking of the times you caught your limit, the big one you caught or the one that got away.

Many parents agree going fishing is one of the best times to be had with a son or a daughter. The day they catch their first fish always brings a smile to a parent's face.

George would take a boat ride sometimes during the blossom time to view the glory of the lake with his kids.

When Bobby was five years old, he went canoeing with his dad on the river flowing through Anytown. After they took the boat out one spring day, he told his pal Smithy the boat was better than the canoe because his dad didn't need to use his arms so much with the motor attachment.

One day soon afterward, Jim and George took Bobby out for a "Fishing Lesson." They tutored him on how to bait the hook on a cane pole, direct the line in the water at different depths and how to set the hook after the bobber showed signs of a fish biting.

Once the line was in the water ten minutes, the bobber went down. Jim and George waited to see how Bobby would react. Bobby became excited but didn't lose his concentration. He struggled a bit but with his Dad's help his efforts were accomplished when a better than average bluegill flopped into the boat. The story of the capture of Bobby's first fish was told many times thereafter. Through the years, Bobby became an excellent fisherman.

Billy and Kathleen followed the footsteps of Bobby, Billy when he was six and Kathleen when she was seven, each catching their first fish. Kathleen's excitement for fishing was not on the level of Bobby and Billy, but all three showed great skills in various venues. Starting at age 16, Billy became an excellent fly-fisherman and competed in contests.

CHAPTER THREE

COACHES JOHN RICHMOND AND BUCK ROSE

John Richmond was a mountain of a man who came to Anytown in the autumn of 1967. He bought a mobile home in the mobile home park. He pretty much kept to himself the first year he lived in Anytown. Nobody knew where he came from.

He just appeared one day.

He drove a Corvair automobile. Some wondered how he wedged himself into the small vehicle and folded himself up to get out. Sometimes he went for walks.

He obtained a job at the Hush Puppy factory. He still stayed away from everyone, including the lunchroom. He always said hello and smiled when someone approached him, but he never carried on a conversation with anyone, maybe because he had a cleft lip. He bought his groceries each week at *J and J Grocery* but never went out socially.

One day when John was at work, some kids peeked in the window of his mobile home. Bobby Stone and George Riley were both part of the group. John had many books placed on two shelves that reached to the ceiling over a goodly portion of his living room. These reading materials consisted of several classics and many sports-related books.

They peeked in until a Saint Bernard dog came loping over and they *chose* to leave the premises.

Then one day in July 1968, John decided to walk down to the nearby park to eat his lunch. A stranger sat on a park bench eating his lunch and John sat down nearby.

The stranger said, "Hello. How is life in the slow lane?"

This went on for a couple of weeks when the weather was pleasant, with the same greeting from the stranger every day. Their conversation eventual advanced beyond the stranger's greeting to, "How is your day going?" and, "Nice weather today."

"Okay," and, "Yes," were John's usual responses.

Then one day after another two weeks, John came over and sat on the bench next to the stranger and asked the stranger for his name.

"You've been speaking to Buck Rose," the stranger said. Buck was an African American man who was named after Buck Leonard, a great baseball player who played in the Negro Leagues and was inducted into the Hall of Fame in 1972. Buck had just moved to the area and was establishing a television sales and repair business which he had opened recently in Sometown, located west of Anytown. Buck had moved to Anytown from the Chicago area. He said it wasn't a good place to bring up his two children Jaden and Jade. Jaden and Jade were eight-year-old twins. He said his wife had been killed in a robbery at grocery store where she worked in August of 1967

Buck said he worked for the sanitation department by day and learned his new skills from a friend of his who owned a television and repair business. Charles, he said, "showed me the ropes of the television sales and television repair business." His friend was a Caucasian man named Charles Frawley Lincoln and they'd played basketball together in high school.

. Buck said after his wife's death, he sold his home in Chicago, took his savings and some benefits he was provided from the market and opened the business in Sometown. He said the owner of the market and his wife had really adored Buck's wife Jewel.

Buck was, to say the least, an outgoing man. He had the ability to make a person believe in what he said right off. He also had the ability to make a person believe in him. Buck liked to sing and write poetry.

Each week, John listened to Buck tell of his background. Then one day he opened up to Buck. He told Buck he'd grown up in West Virginia, the son of a coal miner. His dad worked in the mines all his life. John played football and basketball in high school. He played basketball at West Virginia University in 1963. He was given a scholarship to attend. He worked both the summers between his freshman and sophomore year and sophomore and junior year at the coal mine, where his dad was a foreman.

His dad convinced him to work at the mine to build up his already rather strong body. One day, a mine shaft collapsed. John saved several lives by holding up a timber while other miners ran to safety. He also carried out several injured miners. He tried to save his dad but to no avail. His father lost his life.

On what became his last trip to save other miners, a timber came down and crushed his leg, and he lifted the timber off himself. Maybe because of shock or just plain guts, he managed to drag himself to a safe location where emergency workers could help him.

He'd had a long road to recovery. His coworkers helped his mom with expenses. The mining company also help him and worked out a settlement for his dad and for his heroic deeds.

His mother died of cancer in the summer of 1966. He said the memories of the of the mine accident, his dad's death and his mom's suffering and death caused him to want him to leave the area of West Virginia where he lived.

He was left with a noticeable limp from his injury.

John said he'd dated some but felt his cleft lip turned off women.

Buck said, "Ah! I think that's all in your mind."

John said he bummed around some, spending the money he'd received from the settlements. He said he had a friend from college who was from Michigan who said Southwestern Michigan was a good place to live, so he'd packed up all his cares and woes and drove around the area, deciding to settle in Anytown because people seem to be the kind of people he needed to be around. He said he walked a lot to try keep his leg built up. Although he wasn't excited about continuing his college education, he did enjoy reading, mostly sports and history literature.

As days went by, Buck and John became better acquainted. They visited each other's homes. They learned from each other that they might wish to coach youth together someday in whatever sport because they shared the same ideals about sportsmanship and coaching methods.

One day Buck shared a poem with John about their friendship.

It went as follows:
You meet a stranger in a park
A guest in your life
A newcomer
A visitor to you
A sojourner
You discuss the weather
You discuss family
You discuss life
Friendship develops
A stranger no more
You become comrades
Steadfast brothers
A unity of fellowship
Steadfast solidarity
A stranger no more

John and Buck basically peeled back the onion on each other.

One day, Buck shared his insights on life. He said, "John, I see the world as it should be. Too many times people place the negative in their daily thoughts. The world doesn't stand still just because you have a bad day. Failure isn't fatal, no more than success is final. Success and failure can weigh heavy on the soul or make you stronger for the everyday of your life. This will give you the courage to continue."

He'd had some successes and some failures. He'd gone to Washington for the *Freedom and Job March* in 1963. He'd had seen some changes in attitudes toward the black man since then, "But it has spread awfully slow."

Buck continued, "I didn't know how the death of Martin Luther King in April was going to play out. Seeing the world as it should be, was all well and good, but living the life of a black person was not yet as the world should be."

Buck and John shared family outings, attendance at sporting events, weddings, funerals, golfing, bowling and card games. They were strangers no more.

As the years progressed, Buck and John became friends with almost everyone in Anytown. Jaden began to call John Richmond Uncle John. John's shyness and Buck's gift for gab played well for individuals in accepting both these fellows. The prejudice of the world didn't seem to exist in the world of Anytown regarding Buck and John.

As the next few years went by, John became more vocal. Buck stated once that John had had a lot to deal with in his life prior to living in Anytown, and now he'd become more open to the good things in life.

Prejudice occasionally crept into their lives from others. Most of the prejudice came from people who didn't know Buck. Seeing John and Buck together seemed to change attitudes. Not a good reason, but sadly true.

Bowling together and golfing together exposed others to what two good people could do to show the beautiful side of life. Alton Jones, (another black man), Earl Fox and David Sanborn were the other members of the bowling team. Everyone enjoyed the whole team and marveled at how well they enjoyed each other. The way they shared jokes and their good attitudes with other teams spilled over for an enjoyable night of bowling for all.

CHAPTER FOUR

BOBBY STONE

Bobby Stone was born in September of 1960. When he was two years old, his dad was changing a tire on truck used on the *Stones Fruit Farm*, when the tire blew up in his face and killed him. His mother grieved for two years. One day in 1964, Connie Stone began seeing David Sanborn, who delivered mail.

Dave was a wonderful guy with terrific sense of humor. He loved to hunt and fish. He loved cinnamon rolls. Bobby's mother liked to bake and was renowned for her cinnamon rolls. Dave stopped over for breakfast almost every morning at the Stone House to enjoy Connie's offerings. He once said to Bobby's mother that a balanced diet was a roll in each hand.

Once when Connie made a negative comment about something, he said people who lived in the Stone house should not throw glass. This didn't go over too big with Connie, but five-year-old Bobby thought it was hilarious, once Dave had explained the humor in his comment.

These comments and others evidently didn't discourage Connie too much and there was a marriage at Niagara Falls in June of 1966.

Being small in stature didn't help Bobby's basketball skills. Shooting wasn't his forte, but bringing ball down the court and defensive ball hawking were the skills in which he excelled. Bobby excelled more as a baseball pitcher. He had a very strong arm and pitching delivery. He struck out ten or more batters on several occasions in his career. As for football, pound for pound, he was a tough middle backer and was very quick.

He and Dave lifted weights together in the basement of the Stone house. A little sister named Carrie came along in 1969. Carrie was a little spitfire who didn't let any grass grow under feet. Carrie loved Bobby and tagged along whenever she could.

Connie was ten years older than Dave. She completed her medical degree 1970 at the age of 36, just after Carrie was born. Bobby's grandfather Charlie Stone was a carpenter and grower. After Bobby's dad Milborne died, Charlie financed Connie's education or her " schooling," as Charlie put it. Milborne was working on one of Charlie's trucks at the time of the accident.

Dave basically did the housework and stayed home with Bobby and later with Carrie after delivering the mail. He also coached baseball beginning when Bobby was eight years old all the way through high school.

Dave had joined the U.S. Army when he was 19 years old. He was Allstate in four sports but he liked baseball best. The Detroit Tigers showed some interest in him, but he chose the service instead because his father Abe was a career serviceman. Dave hurt his arm while playing in a pick-up game while in the service and the arm never came back. When he returned, the Postal Service provided a good job.

His brother Don joined the service in 1964. He attended Central Michigan University, Mt. Pleasant Michigan, where he played right offensive guard on the football team. The Green Bay Packers showed some interest but he never completed his degree in education. Instead, he became a member of the Green Berets.

Don was killed in June of 1966 in Vietnam, leaving a wife and three children behind, including his son Dick, who was nine at the time. Don's wife met another military man from the navy and moved to Virginia Beach, Virginia, But Dick spent every summer with David until he was eighteen. Then he returned to Michigan and attended college at Kalamazoo College.

Carrie was stationed at Virginia Beach a year later when she joined the navy.

CHAPTER FIVE

JADEN ROSE

J aden was the star of the basketball team. He averaged 18 points per game with an average of 10 to 12 rebounds per game plus four to six assists per game. He was a 6'8", 210 pounds of muscle and brawn. Jaden was also the tight end on the football team. He set records which were not all recorded because some stats weren't kept in those days.

In 1974, Jaden showed some of his athletic ability when he and Bobby Stone led their baseball team to a championship and two tournament championships in the local summer baseball league. When Bobby Stone wasn't pitching, Jaden threw a few innings in games. He had the outstanding ability to hit a baseball to all parts of the diamond. Jaden received a scholarship to play both basketball and baseball at Western Michigan University.

In July of 1981, after graduating from college, he married his high school sweetheart from Sometown, Sherlee Brown. Sherlee was Jaden's sister's best friend. Sherlee and Jade had met at summer camp between seventh and eighth grade and became friends thereafter. They served as cabin leaders in different cabins the summer prior to their senior year.

Jade worked at her father's business as a salesperson and helped him repair televisions. Jaden received his Bachelor's Degree Economics in June of 1981 and his Master's Degree in Economics in January of 1983. He obtained a position thereafter at Edward Jones, which was expanding their financial services.

Sherlee and Jaden had an addition to their union. Diana Ross Rose was born in January of 1983. Willie Horton Rose was born in March of 1984. They built a home overlooking Lake Michigan in 1989.

Gerry Martin

CHAPTER SIX

TIMOTHY CLAUSEN (TIMBO)

t was a December day in 1973 at Saint John's High School in Kalamazoo, Michigan. Ed Clausen was an eighth-grade teacher at the parochial school. Ed was putting his junior varsity basketball players through their paces. Ed had dreamt of coaching and teaching at this school when he was in in ninth grade himself. The enrollment at the school was 946 students between elementary and high school. Ed's teams played freshmen and junior varsity teams in the area.

"Run the play," shouted the 44-year-old coach. He blew the whistle attached to his wrist to stop the action so he could give further instructions. "Wake up, Timbo," he called to his son. "You need to post up on that play. We learn by reaction." Practice continued through the remaining portion of the hour-and-a-half of time, with the boys taking the coach's comments with good-natured respect.

"Remember, you can do whatever believe you can do," Ed related. "You must condition yourself for the long run!"

Near the end of practice, as the boys completed their final laps around the gym, coach Ed relaxed in his wheelchair. Ten years earlier, a car accident had shattered the fourth and fifth vertebrae of Ed's spinal cord. Although confined to a wheelchair ever since, Ed progressed to fulfill his dream of coaching and teaching.

He was an inspiration to his students, players and all those with whom he came into contact.

In March of 1975, John Richmond interviewed for the job of coaching the varsity basketball team at Anytown. The varsity coach George Hyatt had left Anytown to coach at Lansing Eastern in Lansing, Michigan. John was hired in April of 1973 to coach the junior varsity. Buck Rose was approved to be his assistant. By the end of the month, John was approved to coach with Buck as his assistant for the 1975/76 season.

One day in April just after his appointment to coach the varsity basketball team, John had a doctor's appointment in Kalamazoo. Ed was in the waiting room. Ed and John had known each other since Anytown had played Saint John's in baseball and basketball. John informed Ed of the opening at Anytown for the junior varsity coaching position. He said Buck had been offered the job but had chosen to work with John because Jaden would be on the varsity team. There was also an opening for a math teacher to teach algebra and geometry.

Since Anytown was five miles from his home and the job would negate driving twenty-five miles to Saint John's, Ed decided to interview. During the interview, Ed stated, "A teacher needs to take a genuine interest in each student and not only plant the seed, but nourish it, as well. Students and athletes should not just survive, but thrive." This statement sealed the deal and Ed was hired.

Timbo was a 6'6", 180-pound young man who ran cross-country with the team, even though he wasn't eligible to run in meets. After the second semester he joined the varsity basketball team. He played forward and he was a hardworking athlete who was well-liked by his peers. Timbo also ran in the 1976 Boston Marathon and dedicated his run his dad. He was in great shape. Ed, John and Buck said he could run forever. His stamina helped him as a great defensive player in round ball.

Timbo and his sister Mandy lived by the strength of their father's beliefs and courage. Both as students and athletes, they were pushed to believe in themselves and because of this, they thrived.

Timbo did get occasionally into mischief. Once he bragged he could eat 12 hamburgers in one sitting. A kid name Seth Wilson challenged him. Timbo ate all 12 and Seth paid for the burgers plus two dollars for the win, although Seth's dad owned the bar and restaurant in town where the deed was performed.

Once, Timbo told some of the members of the basketball team he could outrun a car from a dead stop to a point he'd chosen. He stopped some kids in a car and told them what he wanted to do. He set the point forty yards away to a telephone pole.

He made eight dollars that day.

Timbo's mother Alice had aspirations of becoming an actress. She enrolled at Western Michigan University for the purpose of learning more about drama. She'd acted in high school plays and in the local playhouse in Three Rivers Michigan.

Alice met Ed in 1952 in their sophomore year of college. They married in 1954. Mandy was born January 9th, 1956. Timbo was born December 12th, 1959. Alice decided to switch her major to education, namely English and social studies. She obtained a job at Perigan High School ten miles from Anytown and Ed and Alice purchased a home there. She was still able to follow her passion when she directed senior plays each year with the band/music teacher. This became a go-to event each year.

Mandy attended Perigan, where she won the State Championship on the debate team with her peers during her junior and senior years. Mandy attended Western Michigan University for two years and then attended Ferris State University in Big Rapids, Michigan, where she graduated from the dental hygiene program. She took a job in a dentist's office in Three Rivers, Michigan, where her mother had grown up.

Mandy married a friend of her cousin's brother. She met him when she debated against his school in Constantine, Michigan. He also came to a family reunion with her cousin's brother when Mandy was in her senior year in high school. His name was Albert Giles. He finished his education to become a lawyer in 1980 and worked at a law firm in Constantine.

Timbo attended Central Michigan University for two years and then transferred to Ferris and enrolled in the physical therapy program. His interest piqued in this program as result of the therapy his dad had gone through after his accident. This was his lifelong career.

Timbo married Mollie Stewart, whom he met at Ferris. Mollie was enrolled in the environmental health program as one the first female students. Mollie obtained a job at the County Health Department in Anytown. Timbo worked at Borges Hospital in Kalamazoo.

Gerry Martin

CHAPTER SEVEN

DALE RICHTER

D ale was born October 6, 1959. Dale's parents were Scott and Camille La Rogue. Camille's father Joseph served a stint in the military in France during WWI. He was a mason most of his life. He performed masonry on several homes in southwestern Michigan.

He was single until he was 42 years old, when Estelle Andres convinced him that he could not live the rest of his life without her. Estelle was a nurse at Saint Luke Hospital in South Bend, Indiana.

Camille was born in 1930, 11 months after her parents were married. Camille married Louis Pullman in 1949. He'd worked for Joseph since he was sixteen. They had two children, Estelle born in 1951 and Doreen in 1952. Two months before Doreen was born, Louis was serving his country in Korea and was killed in battle.

Camille was left alone to raise two daughters. Joseph died in 1954 from a heart attack while splitting wood. Camille's mother helped as much as she could. She took care of little Estelle and Doreen while Camille work at the local winery. After Joseph passed, Estelle moved in with Camille and the girls in a home Camille had purchased with a government loan.

Scott La Rogue graduated from Nearbytown High School in 1948. When he was sixteen years old, he worked in the at *J and J's Grocery* owned by Harold Jones and Elmer Johnson. He worked as a bagger.

A few months after he graduated, he learned the skill of a butcher from Mr. Jones, as he forever referred to him. Elmer and Harold understood their business was growing so they decided have Scott assist Harold. They really liked Scott as a person and appreciated his work ethic. He was always willing to do any job he was asked to do. Scott's dad owned one of the local grain elevators and feed mills.

Scott chose to enter the U.S. Army in 1955 and was stationed in Germany soon after. Camille advanced to manager of the winery in 1956. During the autumn of 1957, Camille was attending a meeting with growers. Scott was on leave after having returned from Germany to the States. He was sitting on a bench just down from the winery smoking a cigarette, a habit he'd picked up after entering the army.

Camille was passing by after the meeting adjourned. She smiled at him. He smiled back. She'd seen Scott around when she was a cheerleader for Anytown and he played sports for Nearbytown.

She asked him, "What are you doing here in Anytown?"

He said, "My dad put me to work at his business. No rest for the wicked."

There was just something about Scott. Camille thought he was special. She commented that he shouldn't be smoking, since she blamed smoking for the death of her father.

Scott said, "I'll probably quit after my stint in the army is done."

They began to talk a little more.

Two days passed by. Scott decided to ask her out and she accepted. On that date, they shared their life history up until that point. A few months went by and they wrote to each other until Scott was discharged from the army. Scott met the girls and Camille's mother, who all loved Scott. They married in February of 1958.

He obtained a government loan and purchased half of *J and J's* as Harold Johnson wanted to retire. Scott's dad also provided some funds for the purchase. Elmer Jones was still a few years away from the age of retirement and wished to maintain ownership. Harold stayed on part-time for a few years. They both showed Scott the workings of running a business. Camille left the winery and began managing a wine tasting and sales restaurant and winery in Saint Joseph Michigan called *Vintage*.

Scott and Camille tried to have child; however, it was discovered after a great deal of testing that Scott was unable to produce offspring.

Scott's best friend Carl Richter and his wife Patty were killed in an auto accident in 1964 and their five-year-old son Dale was left without parents. Scott and Camille were named in Carl's will to take Dale into their home, since they were Dale's godparents for baptism in the Catholic Church. They adopted Dale.

Dale didn't have a lot of interested in sports. He liked to toss horseshoes, but mostly liked to read and study history. Scott never pushed him into sports. He was a close friend of Jaden Rose and George Riley, and they often talked him into playing basketball with them and others. Dale was 6'1" and one-hundred-seventy-six pounds. He could jump and had a dead-on shot from the corner.

As time went on, his interested piqued in playing the sport. Most of time, though, he worked at his dad's store or at his grandpa's business and concentrated on his schoolwork. When Dale was in eighth grade, Scott put up a basketball hoop in the barn on their 80-acre property used to harvest blueberries. Scott's friend Ernie Hill ran this operation and his own operation.

Many times, even with the hoop in the barn, Dale had to be coaxed into playing pick-up ball. Dale seemed to enjoy performing in high school games but was a bookworm most of the time.

Scott and Camille didn't discourage him.

The barn and acreage also provided Doreen and Estelle the ability to raise beef for the County Fair every year. Estelle obtained a degree from Ferris State University in food service management in 1970 and a degree in business in 1972. Thereafter, she managed the restaurant portion of the *Vintage*. Camille was now head of operations.

Doreen obtain a degree in business at Ferris in 1973. She worked at a bank in Big Rapids and eventual became the bank manager. They used their money from the raising of beef along with help from their parents to pursue their further educations. Scott and Dale took on the work with the beef when the girls were away to college.

Gerry Martin

CHAPTER EIGHT

THOMAS DECKER (THOM)

O n June 12, 1959, Thomas Dickerson was born with Rh- blood factor concerns.

After the required four-day stay in the hospital were completed, Irene was given the okay to go home; however, Irene could not leave her baby's side, especially since medical staff indicated he might not live many days.

Charles needed to be at his position as president at the nearby Old Fort Bank of Thomasville. Irene and Charles had a seventeen-year-old daughter Rita who attended Western Michigan University. She didn't have any problems at birth.

Thom was a surprise in more ways than one. Each day was a stressful experience for Mom and Dad. He seemed to improve one day and then fall dad back for two days. This continued until July 20th thru 27th when Thom continued to improve each day forward.

A gentle child, over the next eight years he grew into a 6'2", 190-pound young man.

Grandmother Josephine took care of Thom during his developing years. Irene and Charles owned a grocery/dry goods store in Thomasville. Josephine was a women's physical education teacher and librarian at Anytown.

Josephine and her husband Jake owned land just a few miles west of Midland, Michigan. Jake was a crusty man who at the age of thirty had the skin of man who'd spent a great deal of his life outdoors—farming, hunting and fishing.

Jake was not a talkative man and was flinty hard, but people knew him to be honest. He was not someone to joke around with at the wrong time. He might laugh, but you had to pick your times to try any levity.

Josephine Hill was a tomboy. She liked pitch horseshoes with the men as a young girl. She ran every day when she could around Centerville, Michigan. She never back down from a boy when they picked a fight with her. Boys like her athletic skills and would ask her to join in their activities.

Jake Decker grew up in Niles, Michigan. He joined the House of David baseball team when he was twenty. The group came to Centerville in July of 1919, and a 19-year-old Josephine caught Jake's eye. Jake usually limited his conversations with women to, "Hi," if they first approached him, but this time Jake provided the first words with a smile and " Hi."

Jake was an all-out rockum-sockum running and defensive style player. A Ty Cobb type player. Josephine was impressed by his hardnosed method of approaching the sport. His aggressive manner mirrored hers. After the game was over, Josephine visited with Jake. Jake decided to take the morning train the next day back to Niles. His teammates casually teased him, but surprisingly, he accepted it with good humor and, "Ah, you guys."

Josephine's aunt Emma ran a small boarding house and Jake stayed there for the night. Six weeks later, Jake and Josephine were married in a ceremony in Centerville. Jake had been working in Benton Harbor, Michigan for a blacksmith. He stayed in Benton Harbor during the week at a boarding house and returned by train for the weekend to Niles.

After they were married, Josephine and Jake moved to the upper level of a home in Benton Harbor. The lower level was occupied by the owner, Theresa Bauer. Josephine helped Mrs. Bauer with daily housekeeping, cooking and other services. They made a quilt together for both Josephine and Jake's bed and another for Mrs. Bauer.

October 19, 1920, Charles Decker was born. October 18, 1920, Irene Baker was born.

In July of 1922, Jake and Josephine decided pack up a tote for each of them and one for Charles and take the train to the Midland, Michigan area. Jake's Uncle George had performed a Vaudeville act at the Mecca Theater in Midland for some years. George had died and left 80 acres of land to Jake. The land was somewhat cleared, with approximately twenty acres of woods and fifty acres of crop land. The other 10 acres was surrounded with a home and outbuildings.

There was small house, a barn and a shed for a 1916 Model-T Ford. The car was still in very good shape.

Jake struggled a bit trying survive being a farmer. He tried planting different crops, but the land didn't yield well. In 1926, he opened a blacksmith shop. That business made a comfortable living for the family. Josephine helped him when she could, but she mostly watched from a distance with Charles. She and Charles did a great deal of adventuring together around the property and beyond, while Jake spent a great deal of his off-time hunting, fishing and trapping. Jake and Charles didn't bond very much.

1927 brought a change in Jake's, Josephine's and Charles's life. James Graves, the owner of *Saginaw Property Company*, asked Jake and Josephine if he could drill a speculation well on their property. Several successful wells followed, and the rest became history .

Jake did more hunting and fishing throughout the Midwest.

Josephine became interested in the sport of golf. She hired a nanny/ housekeeper/cook. She played every course that would allow her to play and became an excellent golfer. Helen Willis Moody, the winner of many tournaments at the time, became her favorite woman golfer. When Charles was fourteen, he took lessons and learned the game. Charles and Josephine now shared the sport.

In 1933, Jake began assisting potential property owners by opening a building and loan agency. Jake's personality seemed to be a huge asset, providing a feeling of trust to all who did business with him. In 1938, Charles entered Central Michigan College with the intention of learning more about the banking industry. He joined his dad in the business in 1942.

Charles married his high school sweetheart Irene Baker in June of 1940. Charles join the U.S. Army and served in France from June 1941 until Oct 1943, when he was wounded.

Jake discovered that oil had been being found around Bloomingdale, Michigan in Southwestern Michigan. He decided to establish a Building and Loan business in the area and have Charles operate it. Charles was more outgoing, like his mother.

Frank and Emma were married in 1918. Men came in most days just to take a break from a variety of toils and just talk and share stories, sitting at tables which Frank provided. A crystal chandelier hung from ceiling that had a fresco painting of a field of wheat and a field of corn. This establishment and the local barber shop were gathering places for the locals, especially during the winter months.

Irene's dad operated a butcher shop and sold pipe tobacco and pipes. Irene and her mom and dad went fishing in the summer and hunting in the fall and the winter. Frank cut wood for the wood stove in the butcher shop and for the baker's home early each fall. Their eighty acres of property was mostly woods, and a river ran through the property. The river supported different types of pan fish. Charles and Irene went swimming in the river during their teen years when Charles was not golfing with his mother.

Rita was born September 22, 1941, when Charles was overseas.

In 1947, Charles and Irene moved to Anytown. Charles was manager of the *Building and Loan* of Bloomingdale established by Jake in 1946. Charles and Irene rented an apartment in Kalamazoo until their home was built near Anytown. Both Jake and Josephine talked Charles into moving to Anytown because they remembered people saying it was a nice area to live when they were first married. An old friend of Jake's now lived there, Curly Mathews, and the barber in town said it was a nice area in which to live.

Irene and Charles living farther away didn't set well with Josephine. An occasional visit wasn't enough for her. She missed her son. For some time, she tried to get Jake to move near their son, but Jake didn't want to leave the *Building and Loan* to be managed by someone else. He enjoyed the area and his clients.

In 1950, Josephine moved to a two-bedroom home near Charles and Irene. Her marriage to Jake had not been going to well for some time. Jake had gone his way and Josephine had gone her way. They seldom did anything together, so they formally separated. Josephine had obtained a position in the Anytown School District as a physical education teacher and librarian in 1951.

Jake did visit Anytown a few times from 1950 to 1960. Two of the times were when Rita graduated from high school and when Thomas was born. Jake would stay at Josephine's home, but they would sleep in separate bedrooms. They talked the most during Thom's troublesome birth because of course they were both very concerned.

Rita was promoted from second grade to fourth grade. She achieved enough credits after her junior year so she could graduate. Rita obtained a bachelor's and master's degree in chemical engineering. She worked for *Deboise Chemical* in Chicago for a year. Then she was sent to the Philippines to work for the company and lived there until 1969. When she returned, she worked for the company in Midland, Michigan.

When Thom was born, Josephine resigned from job at Anytown High School to take care of him. When Thom was 10 years old, Charles and Josephine took him out to learn how to golf. Josephine did most of the teaching of the mechanics of the game, as Charles lost most of the function in his left arm from the wound he'd received in the war.

By 1967, Jake and Josephine had regenerated their marriage. They became frequently visitors to each other.

In 1969, Jake decided to retire from banking business. The *Building and Loan* had become *The Saint Charles Bank* in Saint Charles, Michigan in 1960.

Jake decided some of his retirement would be spent working at the *Bloomingdale Savings and Loan,* which had developed from the *Building and Loan.* He moved in with Josephine at this time.

Charles had left the Bloomingdale location in 1958 to take the position of president of the Thomasville bank.

The first item on Jake's retirement plan was to discuss the art of baseball and football with Thom. Basketball skills were learned in the junior high program.

At this time, Josephine and Jake decided to help others by making gifts to various groups. They wished to share some of their wealth. They gave $5K to the Methodist Church for a renovation project they were conducting. If money was needed for some community project, they were more than happy to give.

Charles, Irene and Thom did the same.

Thom's friends sometimes had to guard against Thom's good-heartedness. One individual who "borrowed" a little too much from Thom, was told by Bobby Stone that the gold rush was over, and the gravy train was at the end of the line. Bobby had heard that line from Dave Sanborn a few times and that seemed like a good place to use it.

Dick Vogel was Thom's best buddy. They'd ridden the bus together since kindergarten. Dick's dad died when he was in his freshman year of high school. Without any insurance, Dick's mother, Dick and his sister Angie had to sell their farm. They kept one acre on which to place a mobile home.

When Thom and Dick were in their junior year, Charles and Irene bought a used 1967 Chevy Biscayne for them to work on. When the work was completed, the car was left in the care of Dick's family. That had been the Irene's and Charles's intent to begin with. Dick's mother was also employed by Irene and Charles at their store.

Dick was not an athlete; however, he couldn't really participate in sports anyway because he had to watch his sister Angie, who was seven years old. After Dick's and Angie's father died, Dick had to perform duties around the house.

Frank Baker wasn't an advocate of athletic participation. Horseshoe pitching and playing all types of cards were more to his liking. He understood the concepts of baseball and basketball. His opinion of football, however, was that young men ran jumping on each other, trying to retrieve an oddly-shaped ball in the hands of one of the young men. People would try to explain to him the more detailed concepts of the sport but he would fluff them away with his hand and say, "I know enough to know I'm not interested."

One day in 1970, his only grandson Thom sat him down and explained football to him. He conceded that it did have more character to it, but still thought it was strange sport.

Like wrestling.

Thom also explained the finer points of basketball and baseball. To Frank, golf was croquet only over a larger area.

Frank's son and his wife Joan lived in Redford, Michigan. They never had any children but they were both teachers.

Emma Stone died in 1972 from lung cancer, yet she never smoked a day in her life. Emma was everything to Frank.

Frank could be crass at times. At Emma's 60th birthday party which he organized, he said, "There are so many candles if we had a power outage, we could light the whole house."

When someone cheated, he said, "They say we come from snakes. I think he or she did not make the change."

He said, "Marriage is an institution. So is prison."

He said, "Will Rogers said he never met a man he didn't like. I have met a few who are odd and strange people."

He said, "If brains were dynamite, that guy would not have enough blow up a glass of water."

A priest died in 1956 who had been in the community from 1920 to 1947. They had a memorial service at his previous parish as he was buried in his hometown, Ludington, Michigan. Someone asked Frank if he was going to the memorial and he said, "I don't think he would have gone to my funeral. Why should I go to his?" Some people would ask Emma how she put up with him. She'd answer, "That's Frank just being Frank. Deep down, he's a wonderful man."

At Emma's funeral, he spoke of his wife. He said, "My tears are overflowing for my Emma. Emma was notorious for her self-sacrifice, caring for others and her unrivaled work ethic. She was a wonderful example for others to live their lives. Her wonderful sense of humor and engaging smile will be missed not only by my children and me, but also by others who knew her."

Frank was crushed when Emma passed away. He basically ate tuna and other foods out of a can and peanut butter sandwiches after her death. He sold his shop. He didn't take care of himself in other ways. His personal welfare went downhill. He didn't keep up the inside and outside of his home.

This went on for almost a year. Finally, Irene and Carl talked him into moving near Irene. They thought Frank would be more comfortable living in Anytown, which was more rural than Redford where Carl lived. Rita Decker purchased his property, which was near her work, anyway.

Irene found a two-bedroom home just inside the city limits of Anytown. After a few months, Irene convinced Frank he needed a cook and housekeeper. Gail Jenkins had lost her husband Albert about the time Frank had lost Emma. She was hired to perform housekeeping duties. She was living in an apartment over the hardware store.

Three months after this arrangement, another arrangement was made for Gail to move into the second bedroom in the home. Irene and Frank hired Gabby Gipson and her dad to build an addition on the home, creating a separate bathroom and private room for Gail. Frank and Gail continued this arrangement for the remainder of their lives. They both remained committed to their lost spouses. They did enjoy each other's company over the years.

CHAPTER NINE

GABBY AND JOHN

G abby Gipson graduated from Anytown High School in 1961. She furthered her education at Central Michigan University in Mt. Pleasant, Michigan. She achieved a bachelor's in education and a master's degree in administration by 1966. In 1967, she began teaching history and social studies at Anytown high school and middle school. In 1974, she became principal of the junior and senior high Schools. Her father Jack and her mother Sherry owned *Jack's Place*, a bar and restaurant in Anytown.

In 1964, Gabby had a personal tragedy. Her boyfriend Chris Chambers was visiting her. He had a pilot's license, and his dad owned a helicopter. He was five years older than Gabby and had served in the U.S. Airforce and was sophomore at Central Michigan University.

It was Sunday morning, and he was going to fly back home near Flint, Michigan, and then he was going to drive back to college in the afternoon. Gabriel was scheduled to fly with him, but her dad needed her to work at their establishment. She didn't have classes on Monday, so she was going to drive back to school the next day. Chris took off out of a field on the Gipson Property. Gabby waved to him as he took off, and he waved back. She watched as the helicopter went down a mile from her house. Chris died in the crash.

Gabby kept to herself for some time. She mourned Chris's death for a long time. For a long time, she didn't date. Between teaching and working for her dad, she avoided romance.

John left his job at the factory in 1971. Tony Ponza had started a vending machine business and told John he needed a partner. Tony and his folks had taken a restaurant that originally seated forty customers near the expressway in Kalamazoo and expanded it into a one-hundred-fifty seat business. His dad Wally and mom Jill also operated a tree nursery. John felt based on the Ponza's successes in business it was worth going in with Tony into the vending business.

Gabby and John had been acquainted with each other for some time, but if they spoke to each other, the conversation was limited to a few words exchanged between them. In 1973, John and Buck would stop in after basketball practice and have a beer at Jack's Place. Gabby would sometimes sit and talk to them when she wasn't busy. She liked to discuss history with John and listen to how they were going to handle coaching the junior varsity basketball team. Gabby also was intrigued with John's thoughts and beliefs because she felt they were similar to hers.

They never went out on a date. Then one Saturday afternoon in August of 1974, they were sitting on a bench in front of Jack's Place when the subject of who could skip a rock across the water with more skips. The challenge was on. They arrived at the public access of Clear Lake and began the contest. After few attempts by both, out of the blue, Gabby asked John, "When are we going to get married?"

John said, "How about next June?"

Gabby said, "Sounds good."

They didn't discuss their plans with anyone. Soon, though, the connection was made that something was afoot when Gabby started visiting John at his home. John had purchased a house with three bedrooms in 1971. Gabby was familiar with the house because she and her dad had built the house in 1969. The previous owners had moved to Cleveland, Ohio for the husband's new job.

Every year since 1967, Gabby and her dad would build a house together. Jack called it bending nails together. They started in mid-April and hopefully finished by mid-August before Gabby had to return to teaching. They would have a buyer prior to building the house.

CHAPTER TEN

CASEY ADAMS

The 1974-75 varsity basketball season concluded with the team record for the year being 13 wins and 11 losses. When completed, the regular season record was 10 wins and 10 losses. The Hawks won their district tournament though they were not favored to win. Coach Hyatt had built his team around point guard Casey Adams for three years. Prior to these years, he coached with more uniform standards where the whole team was included into shooting the ball. Coach Hyatt had coached at Anytown since 1964 and was well liked.

Casey had score 48 points in one game and had several games where he scored over 30 points. Many of his attempts would have been considered three-point shots when they became part of the game in later years. He scored several points driving to the basket, but his favorite shot was from the outside.

The Hawks won the first two games of the district with close games against equal competition. The district final pitted the Hawks against Sometown. They had one 6'10" young man named Earl Mogg and one 6'11" young man named Gene Moore. Both players had dominated the game throughout their high school careers, rebounding and scoring underneath the hoop. They were known as *M & M Twins*.

This particular night, 5'10" Ed Ponza and 5'11" Paul Zepetski boxed the gentlemen out the whole night, out rebounding the "Twins" offensively and defensively. They managed to alter their shots, equaling causing problems with their scoring points. Casey Adams also scored 31 points, which definitely helped the cause. The final score was 54 Hawks to 49 Comets. This was especially nice because the Hawks had lost to Sometown 80 to 49 during the regular season.

The first game of the regionals was with Martinville. Casey Adams could not make a basket shooting from the outside and they team double-teamed him when he drove to the basket. This caused him to fail to make the closer in shot. Casey scored only 10 points for the night. Sophomore Jaden Rose scored 20 points, mostly from grabbing offensive rebounds. The team seemed lost because Casey was not hitting his shots. They lost the game 51 to 44.

Even though Casey was the star of the team, he was not well liked. He was definitely not a leader. When he made a basket, he'd run back down the floor with two fingers in the air. This didn't set well both with the opposing players and the Hawks fans. He often didn't correctly get back on defense as a result of his actions.

Fans and his teammates were embarrassed by Casey. They were also concerned that Coach Hyatt let him get away with his actions. When approached about this situation, Coach Hyatt said his action helped him stay focused. Many disagreed, and Coach Hyatt lost some of the respect he'd had before Casey became part of the team.

Casey would tease underclassmen in every sport he played (also football and baseball). He bawled out these athletes when they made mistakes. His teammates would get his wrath when many times he was just as much at fault for the mistake. He was very careful to not perform these actions around coaches and other adults.

He gave Jaden Rose a lot of static when Jaden was brought up to varsity halfway through his freshman year. Jaden told his dad. Buck mentioned it to Coach Hyatt. Coach gave the standard answer he always gave. "I never saw or heard Casey do that."

The strange thing about Casey was in the classroom he was a model student and never spoke much to anyone.

His father was a barber in Nearbytown. The young boys liked him. He always spoke to them kindly and asked about what was happening in their lives. Everette Perkins was the barber in Anytown. He'd taken over the business from Curly Mathews in 1953 when Curly decided to become a minister. Everette basically just cut hair and spoke little. Older men went to him because even though he spoke little, he did encourage discussion in his shop, and he attended all sporting events and gave to school projects. Casey's dad never attended any athletic events he played in.

Casey left town two days after his graduation. Some said he may have enlisted in the army. No one ever heard from him again.

Casey's dad died from a heart attack in 1989. Casey's mother told people a few days after the funeral that Casey's dad physically beat both of them.

CHAPTER ELEVEN

THE LEADUP

November 14th began the basketball season for the 1975-76 season. Edwin Ponza, Casey Adams, Paul Zepetski, Larry Thomas and Gail Brown had graduated from the 1974-75 team. Seniors Kyle Andrews and Jacko Prine and Junior Jaden Rose were holdovers who contributed the most to that team. Kyle Andrews was the other guard with Casey Adams during the prior year.

Buck and John had discussed the possible starters beyond Jaden Rose, who would start at center. Forwards would be Dale Richter and Thom Decker. The point guard would be Kyle Andrews and the other guard Jacko Prine. George Riley would go in for Kyle when need be. Bobby Stone would go in for Jacko when need be. Bo Washington, a sophomore, would go in when needed for the other three starters up front. Bo was a good defensive player and rebounder, but his scoring skills, not so much. Timbo Clausen would spell all players when needed when he became eligible during the second semester.

The first practice was devoted to John and Buck discussing with the team expectations for the coming year. They said the team would play a box and one defense. They stressed that every player on the team would be of value to possibly putting the ball through the nets. Buck said, "We'll be working the ball to get a good shot, but don't be afraid to shoot if you have an open shot."

Over the years, John had gathered information from articles and the like provided by Ed Tucker from Cincinnati University, John Wooden from UCLA University, Branch McCracken from Indiana University and Adopf Rupp from Kentucky University. John and Buck used some of this information to guide the team through the season. Gabby thought, when listening to them, they were on the right track.

Both John and Buck tried to stress the importance of being in shape. They felt with the talent available they could outlast the opposition in the fourth quarter with endurance as a result of being able run the floor easily at this time.

John and Buck told the team that in following days they would be running defensive and offensive strategies. They said the offense and defense should be second nature to the players. After the season began, they would be reviewing mistakes and would be practicing free throws. John said, " The ability to make your free throws can be the difference in winning a close game." John said when he was a player, his team made 13 out of 14 free throws in a game and won the game 72 to 69."

John continued, "We'll learn from our mistakes. Turnovers are the key. Some coaches agree that a turnover can be worth a point a game; therefore, if our opponent has 14 turnovers and we have seven turnovers it's worth seven points for us."

Buck stated that many coaches also said "Defense and rebounding are75% of the game. Of course, scoring points is the main objective, but defense and rebounding can win a game when you have a cold night shooting."

Those members of the team who had been on the junior varsity had heard similar statements from Buck and John.

The first game of the season, Kyle Andrews found himself in foul trouble immediately in the first quarter. George Riley came into the game and made 14 straight shots. He could not miss. He ended up with 32 points. This was the best game of George's career by far scoring wise. The final score was Anytown 70 and Livingston 58.

The next practice after this game, John said, "When someone gets as hot as George did, we'll continue to ride that horse every time."

The next four were won by a good margin—80-48, 82-53, 78-45, and 83-49. The sixth game was a struggle against Sometown, although the Hawks came out on top 60-57. The *M & M Twins* had graduated, but they were still a better-than-average team.

Athletic Director Jim Cowens scheduled a Christmas tournament in 1973 to be played the 75/76 season. Those who participated were Nearbytown, Carterville, Anytown and Orangeville. Orangeville was from Indiana. They were runners up in the Indiana State Championship In 1970. Anytown defeated Carterville 70-48. Orangeville defeated Nearbytown 80-46.

The championship game between Orangeville and Anytown was a tough battle. The Hawks were down 23-19 in the opening quarter. Slowly in the second quarter, Anytown started to take the lead. They took the lead 39-38 when Jocko Prine stole the ball and completed full court layup. They held the lead at halftime 46-44. Orangetown carried momentum throughout the third quarter and led 65-62 at the end of the third quarter. The fourth quarter belong to the Hawks. They outlasted the Pirates for a final score of 84-78. During the next practice after the holidays, John and Buck made sure the team was aware they'd won because they were in shape. The Hawks won the next four games handily.

Timbo Clausen became eligible to play the second semester. He was a worthy addition to the team.

For the 13th game, the Hawks traveled to Sometown for a rematch. The Comets were out to revenge the prior losses in the district. During the first meeting, both the teams played intense defense and both teams had trouble getting any momentum offensively. The lead went back and forth throughout the game. Both teams were in excellent shape, fighting tooth and nail in the fourth quarter. Sometown came out on top 56-55 when Art Wesaw, the Sometown point guard, hit a jump shot with two seconds left in the game for the win.

John told the radio station that covered games in the area, the team would reload and regroup.

The next practice, John and Buck told the team they were proud of both teams' sportsmanship, shaking hands and patting each other on the back after a hard-fought game.

John said, "We'll learn from this loss that we need to be aware that we won't breeze through this season. We'll possibly have games like this in the future."

However, the next seven games weren't close. The Hawks average wins were by 20 points. Dale was averaging 12 points and eight rebounds per game, and his shot from the corner was deadly. Thom was averaging 15 points and 10 rebounds per game. Jaden Rose was averaging 22 points and 14 rebounds per game. John and Buck were rotating George, Timbo, Thom, Dale, Bo, Bobby, Kyle and Jocko in and out of the line-up in the last seven games.

*

Everette Perkin's barber shop was the meeting place for discussion of the good fortunes of the Hawks as result of the basketball team's winning ways. Everette and Frank Baker had become friends and attended games together. They always sat near Irene, Charles, Jake and Josephine.

Frank spent a few hours each day sitting at Everette's place. They ate lunch together most of the time. After lunch, Frank would have two beers at *Jack's Place* than go home and watch soap operas with Gail.

Frank had a few comments for the referees in close games. Thom told his dad, "Maybe I shouldn't have explained the game to grandfather."

Daniel Riley made a few comments also regarding the expertise of the officials a few times over the years.

When discussions took place in his shop, Everette would say, "You bet," when a positive remark was made.

Jack Gipson said, "That Everette sure can talk," when one day a few men were speaking of Everette and his very small contributions to the conversation regarding the basketball team. The area in around Anytown was excited about the nineteen wins and one loss regular season.

Jack's Place was busy after games. Jane Vogel had taken a job a *Jack's Place*, working three nights a week in addition to working at Irene's and Charles's business.

Friday night when the team played their last game of the regular season, *Jack's* was packed. A couple came in at 10:30 P.M. They sat down on two stools at the bar after two people left. After a period of time, the couple started a conversation with Mrs. Vogel whenever she wasn't busy. She discussed her life past and present. They told her they lived in Chicago and were visiting friends at Clear Lake. They told Jane they were impressed with her wonderful personality and approach toward life, especially with what she had been through and her present circumstances.

Jane told them life had its ups and downs. She said, "Being positive throughout the day has helped me deal with any troubles and keeps me going. Also, the people of Anytown have been wonderful to me." They shared a few more thoughts. After they left and Jane went to clear the area where they were sitting, she found eight fifty-dollar bills under their napkins. When she asked around and gave people a description of the couple, no one remember seeing both of them before around town, nor out at Clear Lake.

*

The Hawks first game in the district was against Sometown. This time the game went completely different. Jaden Rose grabbed 18 rebounds and scored 22 points. Dale Richter had 14 rebounds and scored 14 points. Thom Decker had 15 rebounds and 16 points. Bobby Stone had one of his best games defensively. The Hawks won 84-52. The next two games were no problem.

The Hawks won their second straight District Tournament. All fifteen players scored in the second game and 12 players scored in the third game. Ed Newton, Pat Simons, Carl Davis, Andy Bailey and Terry Cowens (the Athletic Director's son) were the remaining members of the team.

The first two contest of the regionals were like the district games with wins by large margins. The Ambel Tigers had won their regional games by close margins. The excitement was building around Anytown, with aspirations of winning a State Championship. Ambel had two excellent guards who could hit the outside shot. The Hawks couldn't buy a bucket most of the time. The bottom of the basket eluded them too many times. The Hawks led at half time 29-27. The two guards were scoring the majority of Ambel's points.

The second half didn't go any better for the Hawks regarding shot attempts or rebound put backs. The score was 50-49 with seven seconds left in the game. Lenny White from Ambel had hit an outside shot with nine seconds left in the game. John called timeout. John wanted to set Dale Richter up for the final shot from the corner, where he had been money all year.

The ball came in from Jaco Prine to George Riley. Riley was in the game because Kyle Andrews had fouled out. George looked for Dale, but he was closely guarded. George found Thom at the key. Thom took the shot.

It went in and then out.

Tears flowed in the locker room and on the bus ride home. It took a couple of weeks for Thom to smile again. Buck and John told the team, "This is when you build your character. Winning is great in life, but losing is when you realize what you're made of. Accepting a tough loss is hard. It may help you to think of what we accomplished prior to the loss. Better times will be coming."

Jaden Rose gained the honor of All-State First Team, was voted All-State Academic First Team and was awarded a number of other area awards for his basketball skills. Thom Decker was voted to All-State Second Team and was given a number of area awards. Dale Richter gained Third Team All-State and was given some area awards.

Jaden Rose took Sherlee Brown, George Riley took Paula Price, Bobby Stone took Lisa Brooks, Ken Schmidt took Jade Rose, Thom Decker took Liz Brooks and Timbo Clausen took Amelia Martin to the Prom.

A number of alumni basketball games were organized to be played March 30, 1976. Thirty-two past graduates signed up to play in the game. These gentlemen were split into four teams. They practiced on two Sundays prior to the game. They played six games. Half of the proceeds from the games, concessions, pie and cake raffles and other raffles went to the Athletic Boosters. The other half went to funding the Bicentennial celebration, which was to be held July 2nd thru July 7th.

The Hawks won 23 and lost five baseball games the spring of 1976. They won their district but lost in the second game of the regionals 1-0 to Westville. Bobby Stone struck out 14 hitters in the regional game. The pitcher from Westville was just as good as Bobby. He gave up two hits. Jaden Rose had both hits. Bobby gave up one hit. The winning run was scored on a questionable walk, a stolen base and two sacrifice flies.

Bobby Stone pitched the majority of the games, with Jaden Rose and Thom Decker tossing some innings also along the way. Jaden batted 480 for the year, Bobby batted 440, Thom batted 420 and Ken Schmidt 400. Bobby gained All-State First Team, Jaden Rose also gained First Team and Thom And Ken were Second Team.

Timbo Clausen won the State Championship in the mile and the 100-yard-dash, a rare feat for both endurance and speed. Dave Sanborn won coach of the year Class "C" division baseball. Jaden won the Athlete of the year award for in his contributions to football, basketball and baseball. Bobby won M.V.P. for baseball, Jaden for basketball and Ken Schmidt for football. Ken ran for 1720 yards.

*

Alice Clausen directed a three-act play based on the early American history. The proceeds were to be provided to the Bicentennial committee. The play was held on a Friday night, Saturday night and a Sunday Matinee in mid-May. The play was well attended; in fact, it was also performed one night during the celebration. Seven-year-old Carrie Sanborn was a hit with her rendition of *Yankee Doodle Dandy* as part of the presentation. Jade Rose also had excellent presentation of The American Trilogy (songs *Dixie*, *Battle Hymn of the Republic* and *All My Trails*).

The community had several other funding projects for the celebration.

On July 6th, Carrie and Bobby Stone were tossing a baseball back and forth in the back yard of Frank Baker's home. Connie her mother, Irene Decker and Gail Jenkins were baking cakes and pies to be sold at the celebration. She was watching Carrie and Bobby out the window of the kitchen. She noticed a lot of chattering from Carrie. Suddenly Carrie fired the ball at Bobby's feet. Connie rushed out to see what had caused Carrie to make that throw.

Carrie indicated that she wanted Bobby to take her down to the park to the celebration. Bobby told her he was going to Kalamazoo with his friends. She said, "Bobby can drop me off down there."

Connie told her she was not allowed go around the area without an adult with her. Connie said, "After I get done with work, I'll take you down there around six. Your Dad is working Bingo, so he can't take you until about six, also."

Carrie exclaimed, " I want to go now!"

With that, Carrie took off down to the park, eight blocks, along with having to cross an intersection within four blocks. Connie sent Bobby after her and told him to tell her dad what was going on.

Dave saw her come running. He told his coworkers he'd be back. He quickly went over and took her by the hand and escorted her back to Frank's house. They met Bobby, and he followed them back. Dave said not a word on the way. Carrie was mumbling something under her breath a few times. When Dave and Carrie reached Dave's intended destination, he told Carrie to take a seat in the garage. He spoke to Connie and then returned to the garage. The first discussion was regarding her anger toward Bobby. Second was her disobedience regarding her mother. And third was her foolish and dangerous decision to run down to the park and worry her mother. He also informed her she might be getting a little too big for her britches as result of the praise she had received for her performance. Years later, she admitted she may have put herself on a pedestal at the time.

The action also earned her not being able to attend the remaining portion the celebration and having to do more chores around the house.

*

On August 16, 1976, at approximately 9:30 P.M., Sherlee Brown, Jaden Rose, Jade Rose and Ken Schmidt had just watched the movie *Rich Man Poor Man* and were heading to Ken's house to go swimming. Ken turned onto the highway, and about two miles down the road, the engine went dead, and the lights went out on Ken's 1969 Dodge Charger. Ken was attempting to start the car back up when another car came barreling down the highway. The other car hit the Charger between the driver's door and the front fender. The impact caused the Charger to roll two and half times and land with the undercarriage against a tree.

Jaden incurred a broken left wrist and some bumps and bruises. Jade had several bumps and bruises. Sherlee, who'd been sitting in passengers side in back, came out with a few bruises. Ken received a broken femur, a broken right arm and a broken ankle. Ken said he didn't remember anything about the accident. Jaden said he remembered spinning, Jade said she remembered the tree approaching very quickly and Sherlee said it felt like a ride at the county fair.

They were all taken to the emergency room at the hospital. Sherlee and Jade were sent home with their parents after treatment after a few hours. Jaden stayed in the hospital for two days. Ken was released after ten days. Ken's ankle had been shattered. He had a long road to recovery. Needless say, his athletic career was over for the 1976-77 season. He had a noticeable limp for many years, until 1994 when a specialist made a correction to his ankle that eliminated his limp.

*

Ken's injury was a blow to the football team, as he was their number one running-back. Jaden moved to running-back and played with cast on till the fifth game.

Ken's dad Leo was the defensive/co-head coach. He resigned to be with Ken when his mother, who was a manager at K-Mart in Kalamazoo, was working. Larry McGuire was the offensive/co-head coach.

John and Buck were appointed to replace Leo.

The first game was with Sometown. The defense was strong, but the offense sputtered. The Hawks came out on the short end at 6-0. Jaden ran for a tough 75 yards. Sherlee teased Jaden that Sometown beat Anytown every year she was cheerleader for Sometown. Bobby Stone, Thom Decker and Kyle Schmidt led the defensive charge. Kyle was Ken's twin brother.

Bobby spent the weekend at Ferris College (soon to be University) in Big Rapids, Michigan. Ferris officials were interested in having Bobby play football and baseball for them. He attended the afternoon football game at Taggert Field between Ferris and Michigan Tech.

He went to a dance on Saturday night and met Theresa Williams. Theresa was from Big Rapids and was in her first year of the dental Hygiene program at the college. They wrote to each other. Bobby thought the world of Theresa and told his buddies he was going to marry her someday.

Her parents were Gerald and Judy Williams. Gerald was in landscaping and had a sewage disposal installation business. Judy was a nurse at *Big Rapids Hospital*. Judy was a great woman who would give and do anything to help anyone. Gerald like to hunt and fish. He bowled in a bowling league.

The second game found the Hawks playing Nearbytown. The offense struggled again without Ken Schmidt, but they eked out a win 12-6. Jaden ran for 130 yards.

The third game was with St. Charles, Michigan, a few miles from Jake and Decker's property. Jake, Jim Cowens, and Bud Largent, athletic directors from both schools, made arrangements in 1972 to play a home game in 1975 and 1976.

St. Charles had won the State Championship in Class "C" in 1975. They defeated the Hawks that year 44-6 on a cold rainy night in October at St. Charles's field. The game held in the afternoon at the Hawks field was much more different, but the Hawks still lost 16-0. Jaden Rose managed to gain 110 hard-fought yards on 36 carries.

A spaghetti dinner was offered to the players for both teams, their parents and fans. This was provided by the local American Legion and Lions Club. Rita Decker attended the game and met Abel Perez at the dinner. Abel had been a teacher at St. Charles for ten years. He became principal of the St. Charles middle school and high school in 1981 and superintendent in 1986. Rita and Abel married in 1979.

The fourth game was the homecoming game. Jaden had his cast removed from his wrist two days before the game. Quarterback George Riley threw three touchdown passes to Jaden Rose. Jaden also ran for 120 yards. Kyle Schmidt scored a touchdown on offense and both he and

Thom Decker intercepted passes and ran them back for touchdowns. The Hawks defeated the Perigan Falcons 36-6. Ken Schmidt attended the game in his wheelchair. The team signed the game ball and gave it to him at the homecoming dance. Jade wheeled him around the floor a few times to different music selections.

The Senior Class won the float building contest. The Theme was *Movies*. They chose *The Silver Streak*. THE HAWKS WILL RUN LIKE A SILVER STREAK AND BLOCK LIKE A TRAIN were the words lettered on the float.

George Riley was chosen King and Mary Klein was chosen the Queen of Homecoming.

Mr. Clausen encouraged his students the week before the week of homecoming to come up with a joke for homecoming week. At the beginning of each class throughout the week, a few students could tell a joke. This was only voluntary, however. Marry Klein quoted her dad when canning foods. "Can everything you can. If can't can everything you can, then eat everything you can't can." Mr. Clausen really like that saying. This joke told by Bobby Stone was chosen as the best:

A man went to get a haircut because he was going to travel to Rome, Italy. The barber asked, "Rome? Why do you want go to that place? It's dirty and crowded." The barber then asked what plane he was taking.

The man said, "United."

The barber replied, "You don't want fly with them. They are always late, the staff is rude, and the planes are old. where are you staying over there?" the barber then asked.

"The International Marriot," the man answered.

"Worst place ever," the barber told him. "They are overpriced, have small rooms and the service is terrible. If you want see the Pope, there will be so many people around you will be so far back that he'll look like an ant."

Six weeks later the man returned to the barber shop. The barber asked how the trip had been.

The man said, "The plane ride was great. They overbooked, so my wife and I were bumped up to first class. The service was wonderful, the hotel was gorgeous, the view was great, and the food was wonderful. As we were touring the Vatican, a guard tapped me on the shoulder and said the Pope sometimes randomly picks out people to have an audience with him."

Stunned, the barber asked, "What did he have to say?"

The man said, "He asked where I got that terrible haircut."

The second best was Jade Rose's joke:

A man goes into the pharmacy and asked the pharmacist for something to put on rash between his legs. The pharmacist says, "Walk this way."

The man says, " If I could walk that way, I wouldn't need the ointment!"

George took Mary out to dinner soon after she told that joke. When the greeter took them to their table, he said, "Walk this way."

They grinned at each other.

*

The fifth game was with undefeated Roseville. The game was another hard-fought game. The score was 12-6 in the Hawks' favor. Jaden Rose caught a forty-yard pass from George Riley. The defender fell down just as the ball was coming toward Jaden. On another play, Bobby Stone hit the Roseville quarterback a blow, he fumbled, and Thom Decker ran it back for a touchdown.

Roseville was on the eight yard-line with one minute left in the game. A pass was incomplete on first down, a run gained to the four yard-line on second down. Another run on third down put them on the two yard-line. Roseville called a timeout. The teams lined up. Buck called their timeout. Buck told the boys that he thought they were going to run a sweep with their best back to the right. Indeed, they did, and Bobby and Jaden stopped him at the goal line.

The coaches for Roseville disagreed, and so did the fans from Roseville. Buck was jumping up and hugging Thom and Bobby as they went off the field. A fan from Roseville yelled a racist remark at Buck. Buck ignored him, but Everette Perkins of all people gave him what-for about poor sportsmanship and racist comments.

The sixth game was with Carterville. The boys from Carterville won 14-12. The place kicker for Carterville was the difference. He was true on both his kicks and the Hawks failed both of their two-point conversions.

The seventh game was with Ambel. A discussion with Larry McGuire and Leon Porter, the football coach from Ambel, prior to the regional basketball game, resulted in the scheduled game to be played at Ambel's field. The victory belonged to Ambel in another tight game 8-6. Jaden Rose's 40-yard run was the only score for the Hawks. Dave and Connie Sanborn, along with Carrie and Bobby, visited the Ferris campus on the next day. Arrangements were made ahead of time to have Bobby travel home with his parents. They also visited the Williams family.

In the eighth game, the Hawks played St. Joseph. Jaden caught six passes, ran for 160 yards and scored five touchdowns. The Hawks won 36-6.

Sherlee was at the game because it was played on a Saturday afternoon. She ran up after the game and told Jaden she loved him.

He said, "I love you, too."

She asked, "Do you love me, or do you love me for the little things I do for you?"

Jaden said, "I love for yourself and that you want to do things for me."

Buck, who overheard this conversation, commented, "Well, the apple doesn't fall too far from the tree as far as your quick response. Well said, my boy."

Buck had recently had a few dates with different ladies, himself. He and Jane Vogel went to a Detroit Lions game on a bus sponsored by the American Legion.

The ninth game was with Cotterville at the Cotterville Raiders football field. Jaden caught three touchdowns passes from George Riley. Kyle Schmidt ran for a 10-yard touchdown. Thom Decker intercepted a pass and ran it in from 35 yards out. George scored from 12 yards out. George ran in three of the two-point conversions and Kyle completed three of the other conversions.

Late in the fourth quarter, Gilbert White, the water boy for Cotterville, was placed in the game. Gilbert was born with Downs Syndrome. An arrangement was made prior to the game by all the coaches from both teams to have Gilbert enter the game toward the end of the game and run the ball a couple times with minimum effort from the Hawks to tackle him.

Since the game was 48-6 at the time, Gilbert was allowed even more leeway. He ran the ball four times from the Cotterville 30-yard-line to the Hawks 10-yard-line. Gilbert ran as hard as he could each time before he was tackled, and when he ran back to the huddle, he was excited. His fifth run, he scored. After the score, he ran with the ball straight to the Cotterville bench and was hugged by each player. The Hawks' players also came over and shook hands with him.

Gilbert was Cotterville coach Ron White's son. He was Mr. White's youngest of eight children. There was ten years' difference in the ages of Gilbert and his next-in-line sibling. All his brothers and sisters attended the game.

John announced after the game that he was going to be a father in June of 1977. The team yelled together, Hip, hip hurrah for John and Gabby."

After the game, Jaden Rose needed his right wrist x-rayed. It was discovered there was some damage to the opposite wrist from the one he injured in the car accident. The doctor determined he'd need a cast placed on it for a short period of time. Jaden said he'd shoot the basketball left-handed then during this period.

Jaden received the honor of second team All-State offense. Bobby Stone and Thom Decker were honored with First Team Defense. All three, plus Kyle Schmidt, received some local honors. Timbo ran cross country and received a number of achievements at local and state events.

Gerry Martin

CHAPTER TWELVE

THE SEASON

When Ken came back to school in late September, Bobby, George Timbo and Ken Schmidt started playing the card game euchre, a card game played frequently in the upper Midwest states by adults, high school students and college students.

They played this card game during lunch hours and after school before football practice. Football practice was always 4:15 P.M. because Coach McGuire couldn't get off work at the milk processing company until 4:00 P.M. Mr. McGuire was a foreman at the plant.

Mary Klein and Amelia (Milly) Martin, who was Timbo's girlfriend, felt Timbo and George should be available more during their time at school. However, they also understood that they wanted to spend time with Ken and help him get through the school day. They therefore drafted Jill and June Riley to play Pinochle, another local popular card game.

For several years, Amelia's grandmother Rosemarie Scott spent two weekends twice a year sitting in front of the grocery/dry goods store in Anytown collecting for the Salvation Army. The Salvation Army was founded by William and Catherine Booth in 1878. William had felt a calling to the help the poor in parts of England. He was first a member of the Anglican Church and then became a member of the Methodist Church, where he became a minister.

In 1855, he met Catherine Mumford at church meeting, and they soon married. Soon afterward, they searched for a church which welcomed all people. In 1865, while delivering a dissertation outside a place called the *Blind Beggar Pub* in a poor section of east England, Booth was asked to lead a series of meetings in a nearby tent. As a result of this meeting, Booth founded a group called the Christian Mission dedicated to providing necessities to the less fortunate and a message of salvation. In 1878, he changed the name to the Salvation Army.

In 1880, a group of members traveled from England to New York and introduced the Salvation Army on American shores. The organization was initially established in Philadelphia, Pennsylvania.

Timbo made a history report regarding the Salvation Army in the fall of his junior year, about the same time he started dating Amelia.

He chose the Salvation Army because he was interested in why Amelia's family was so involved with the organization. As result of his research conducted about the family, he got to know Amelia better.

Basketball practice was held as soon as the team was dismissed from school, so euchre was suspended after school. They still played it with Ken during lunch time. Timbo, George and Bobby taught Banjo Brown the game so they could play it on the bus to road games. There were 12 members of the 1976/77 team—Jaden, George, Dale, Bobby, Timbo, Thom, Bo Washington (now a junior), Gary Maeder (a junior), Ed Newton, Pat Simmons and Terry Cowens (three seniors) and Leslie Banjo Brown (a junior).

Banjo was called Banjo because he'd been playing the banjo in a bluegrass band with his family since he was fourteen. He and his family had played at the Bicentennial celebration. Buck and John provided the same essential directions for the coming season as they'd done the previous season for the benefit of Banjo and Gary. They said the team would now be running both a zone defense and a man-to-man defense. They felt man-to-man would be an advantage if opponents started hitting from the outside. They also indicated they would be employing a trap defense off and on when they signaled in order to implement the defense.

John told them he and Buck felt everyone on the team was capable of hitting a bucket. He said, "We're going to take each game one at time and not be overconfident."

The first game was a trip to Martinville, which was officially over when the first quarter was complete. The starting lineup was George, Bobby, Jaden, Thom and Dale. The Hawks led 26-8 at that moment. Jaden Rose even scored six points shooting with his left hand. The low Martinville point total could be credited to the domineering Hawks defense. The second quarter was more of the same as the Hawks led at halftime 42-18. The score was 62-28 when the third quarter ended. Bo Washington and Timbo had been subbed in throughout the first three quarters. During the fourth quarter, Buck and John placed Ed, Terry, Banjo, Gary and Pat on the floor. The conclusion of the game rendered a score of 80-44. Jaden led the Hawks in scoring with 22 points, Dale and Thom had 16 points and Bo had 10 points.

In the second game, the Perigan Falcons came into the game attempting to slow down the pace of the game. Three minutes in, John called timeout and challenged the young men to remain composed and be locked in defensively. At times, the Falcons would try to drive to the basket, but the Hawks put up a defensive wall and remained disciplined. After the Falcons' lengthy possessions, the Hawks would hold them to one shot by grabbing the defensive rebound. After drawing a couple of offensive fouls, the Falcons started shooting from the outside. The final score was 48-26. Dale led the scoring with 12 points. Timbo and Thom had eight points each.

The third game the healthy rivalry between Sometown and Anytown continued in the Anytown gym. The 1974-75 games came back to roost, only this time the Hawks possessed the height advantage. The tallest member of the Comets was 5'10". The Hawks' frontline players averaged 6'5". On this evening, the Hawks' long-distance circuit was busy in the first quarter. George and Bobby hit four shots apiece from downtown. Jaden, Thom and Timbo consistently gathered rebounds on both ends.

The Hawks led at the end of the first quarter 26-10. John rotated Timbo, Dale, George, Bobby, Bo Thom and Jaden throughout the game until three minutes to go in the third quarter, when the score had reached 67-36. He then placed Ed, Terry, Banjo, Pat and Gary into the game. The final score found the Hawks winning 85-58. Dale lead the Hawks with 14 points while Thom, Bobby, George and Jaden had 12 points apiece.

The fourth game John started Thom, Dale, Jaden, Thom and George at the Carterville gym. John shuttled Bo and Bobby in and out of the game during the first half. Carterville trailed the Hawks 56-30. The Carterville five stayed with the Hawks until the Hawks increased their defense after a timeout called by John and Buck with three minutes to go in the first quarter. The Carterville five lost their composure in the second quarter, allowing easy baskets. The Hawks controlled the pace of the game. Bobby had a number of steals for quick, uncontested baskets. Jaden went to the basket strong with his left hand and scored 18 points. The whole team contributed to the outcome of the game. They all chipped in for the final score of 89-51.

In game five, the Hawks entertained the Brownsville team in the Hawks gym. In the locker room before the game, John told the team that Brownsville played with a sense of urgency. They liked to quickly pass the ball around the perimeter and attempted find the open man down low.

Buck indicated that the team would be operating with a tight zone defense. Buck said, "Mr. Richmond may be substituting freely every three minutes. They have equal height to our team at each position. They like to get ahead early and run a fast break when they can do so. Bobby will start at point guard and Timbo will start at the other guard. Both Bobby and Timbo will need to get back on defense quickly if Brownsville grabs the defensive rebound. Both Bobby and Timbo have the speed to keep their guards at bay. Jaden, Thom and Bo will also start the game."

John said, "If we are ahead at the three-minute mark I'll send George and Dale into the game. If not, we'll just send Dale in for Bo. The other four will need to be workhorses."

The two teams stood their ground defensively. A half-court shot at the buzzer by the Brownsville point guard tied the game 18-18 at the end of the first quarter. A back and forth second quarter ended with Brownsville on top 30-28. The third quarter was much of the same hard work defensively by both teams. At the end of the third quarter, the score was 40-38. John started substituting players in and out throughout the fourth quarter. The Hawks held a 50-44 advantage with two minutes left in the game. At this point, the opposing team fouled the Hawks. The Hawks were eight for eight from the free throw line. The final score recorded was 58-46.

After the game, Buck and John reminded the team of the rewards of being in shape and successfully making free throws. The team went to the Decker home, where they sang songs to the accompaniment of Banjo on the guitar and banjo.

*

Ernie Scott's dad William was a minister for a small nondenominational church in a place called Culver Station in the late 1800's, with a congregation of 150 individuals. At that time, it was a busy rail stop to send lumber to Lake Michigan ports, which were then shipped by boat to Chicago, Boston and New York City. This was rich timber which was milled in the Culver area. In those days, Culver Station was also a center for transportation of valued agriculture and horticulture items. The railroad was used for canned and packed foods.

In the 1930's, the railroad industry declined through the area due to lumber being scarce. People moved away from Culver. A grocery store existed until 1952. By 1972, all the structures were torn down except two that were so dilapidated that it was hard to tell what had existed in the building. They were soon after torn down. A roadside park was established with picnic tables and grills at the location. They placed two large plaques in the center of the park stating the history of Culver. Amelia and Timbo had a picnic there a couple of times.

Since 1956, Ernie Scott, Amelia Martin's grandpa, had acted as Santa Claus, one Saturday at *J and J's* in Anytown and one Saturday at Charles and Irene's place in Sometown. From 1965 to 1968, Thom, George and Bobby at one time or another visited Santa Claus and received a candy cane. On August 17, 1966, Fess Parker, posing as Davy Crocket and Daniel Boone, came to visit Kalamazoo. 14 children, including George, Thom, and Bobby, rode the bus driven by Ernie to the Kalamazoo Airport to greet Mr. Parker. Thom, George and Bobby had Daniel Boone lunch boxes. Amelia Martin and Mary Klein were also in the group, but this was of no concern to Timbo and George. Timbo, George and their buddies thought girls had cooties in those days.

Ernie died on August 2, 1976. The whole community mourned his passing.

Timbo decided to replace Ernie as Santa Claus. He acted the part the two Saturdays prior to Christmas at the stores where Ernie had once performed the service.

Timbo, George and Mary sang the Christmas song *Oh, Holy Night* in the Catholic church in Anytown, St. Michaels, at the midnight mass.

*

The second annual Christmas tournament pitted Orangeville against St. Joseph and Anytown against Mr. Clausen's school. Orangeville defeated St. Joseph 78-41.

In the Anytown and St. John's game, the Hawks went on 16-4 run in the first quarter. When the quarter was complete, the score was 24-6. All twelve Hawks played in the game. Buck and John worked different combinations of players into the game. The final score was 76-38.

Timbo jokingly said, "If I'd been playing for St. John's, the game would have closer."

Bobby replied, "No doubt, but if I'd guarded you, you would have earned your points."

The Orangeville and Anytown game began as a physical game which was loosely called by the officials in the first half. As play progressed into the second half of the game, it became even more intense.

Jaden Rose had his cast taken off three days before Christmas. He and Thom Decker were a dominant force around the hoop, but so was Andrew Cooper and Scott Harris from Orangetown. Both teams' guards were active inside and outside with the ball. The score at halftime was tied 40-40. The Hawks had a one-point lead at the end the third quarter, 56-55.

Jaden, Thom, Dale, George and Bobby came out with a purpose both offensively and defensively in the fourth quarter. The Hawks out-pointed the Orangeville five 16-8. Orangeville lost their composure and started turning the ball over. Free throws came to the forefront, and the Hawks made eight out of eight free throws. At the end of the game, the score read Hawks 80, Orangeville 67. Jaden Rose had 24 points, Thom Decker had 20 points and Dale Richter had 18 points. Bo Washington and Jaden both had 14 rebounds apiece.

The eighth game was with Roseville, which was thirty-five miles from Anytown. Nature stepped in about 20 miles from Roseville, creating difficult visibility for driving. By the time the bus arrived at the Roseville's gym, the snow was even heavier. Not even the power of referees can sometimes mean anything. When the game's officials pulled up to the back door of the gym, a staff member was present guarding the area. One of the officials asked if they could park their car by the door so they didn't have to park their car in the lot and walk around to the front of the school.

The staff member held his ground and said, "I have my orders. There is no way that I can allow that."

One of the referees pressed him, saying, "We'll get soaked walking from the parking lot!" The referee knew the gentleman wasn't going to budge and accept their pleas. However, he said, "Let us in and we'll give Roseville a couple of calls."

The staff member didn't crack a smile as they left, since he clearly found no humor in the comment. After all, he was standing in the snow and getting wet.

Jim Klein, the Anytown bus driver, pulled in soon afterward. He opened the door to the bus and asked if the boys could be left off at the same spot. The staff member declined the request, mumbling something about black kids on the bus. Offended by the comment but rising above the insult, John and Buck told the boys, "I guess we walk."

The Hawks fans still had some negative thoughts regarding Roseville and the Hawks football game and Roseville's bad sportsmanship. Roseville had much more talent playing football than basketball. The Hawks were much quicker than a slower-moving Roseville five. The Hawks outran, out-rebounded and outshot them. The final score was the Hawks 58-34. The guards were very deliberate with the ball throughout the game and John substituted freely so as to not run up the score.

The junior varsity game had the same outcome as the varsity game, with Mr. Clausen using the same strategy of substituting and deliberate play, with the final score of 43-21. The trip home was difficult due to the weather conditions, but the Hawks arrived back to Anytown safe and sound. Buck, John and Mr. Clausen told both Anytown teams that the good sportsmanship on their part brought them home safely.

The ninth game was with Cotterville at the Hawks gym. John told the media, "We didn't play our best in this game, but we shot well from the free throw and took good care of the ball, and that made a difference. We took it to them in the first quarter, and after that we made our shots around the floor enough to keep the lead."

The Hawks played good defense. The Cotterville five played better defense than they showed the ability to score on offense. The Hawks were successful in making 18 out of 19 free throws. Also, the defensive boards from John, Thom, and Timbo made a difference. Thom took a bit of ribbing for missing his one free throw. The final score in this game was 65-56.

The tenth game was with Gaither Christian at the Gaither gym. Gaither Christian established athletic programs at their school in the fall of 1974 after having established the school in 1969. Their coach Emery Nelson was hired because of his ability to take struggling teams to more than respectable records over a short period of time. He had this type of success with Ludington, Michigan, Detroit Eastern and Bridgemeir. Bridgemeir was located between Kalamazoo, Michigan and Battle Creek, Michigan. Coach Nelson won a State Championship with Bridgemeir in 1968.

That year when Bridgemeir played Anytown, coach Hyatt's team didn't have a great deal of talent. Coach Hyatt did a good job with the players he had, getting the most out them as was possible. Coach Nelson substituted freely in that game, and as a result, Anytown was more competitive. The final score was 50-36.

Coach Nelson at Gaither Christian had two juniors, seven sophomores and six freshmen. From the get-go, John decided to return the 1968 gesture from coach Nelson. He started George at point guard, Ed Newton, Banjo Brown, Terry Cowens and Pat Simmons. He had Gary Maeder substitute for George for extensive time periods. He sent the other members in one at a time to give the starters a minute's rest.

Kyle Schmidt had joined the team after Christmas. Kyle had been helping his brother Ken. Ken was now walking with crutches and John let Kyle be with his friends with the understanding that his playing time would only be if the team had a substantial lead. Kyle scored a basket after two attempts, set up by John to have George get him the ball. Kyle was an excellent football player, but his basketball skills weren't in line with his football, track (shot put and discus) and baseball (catcher) skills. The final score was 46-36.

In the eleventh game, the Hawks played Martinville at home. The Hawks immediately established momentum by scoring the first four buckets, with the score at the end of the first quarter being 20-8. John and Buck were concerned about the boys coming out flat because the starters didn't play together against Gaither Christian. The two practices before the game were a little longer because the junior varsity scrimmaged with the varsity throughout both practices. This was done to make sure both teams were fresh for their Friday night game.

The Martinville five came out in the second quarter with some pep in their step. The Martinville forwards hit three shots from the corner and the guards hit two baskets apiece in five minutes. However, Bobby stole the ball for two easy baskets, Jaden Rose made three shots down low and, Dale Richter hit three shots from the corner. Neither team missed a shot throughout this time period. This brought the score to 30-20. During the next three minutes, the Hawks out-pointed the Falcons 8-4 for a halftime score of 40-24. With four minutes left in the third quarter the score was 52-28. At this point, John pulled the starters and during the remaining portion of the game, John shuffled in all 13 players in different combinations. The finale score was 70-40.

The twelfth game was with Perigan at the Falcons gym. A young gentleman named Chuck Burns had transferred from St. Phillips High School in Dayton, Ohio. He was 6'11" and 210 pounds. His father was hired as the Superintendent at Perigan in July of 1976. His mother had been born in Sometown and was happy to move back to the area. This was his first game after sitting out a semester. John, Buck and the team had no history of his play other than what Mrs. Alice Clausen said. She mentioned that he was a senior, he was first team All-State in Ohio, and he looked awesome in practice.

The slow-down tactics weren't in the cards as it had been in the first meeting. Their two sophomore guards had now gained experience and had also gained confidence in their shooting and handling of the ball. Plus they now had a dominant player. John, started Bobby, Dale, Thom, Dale and Jaden. Buck's strategy was to double-team Chuck with Jaden and Thom.

Mr. Burns still managed to be a threat with the ball. The guards fed Chuck the ball and he took it to the hoop successfully four times and scored eight points out of the first ten points the Falcons scored. He also shut down Jaden a bit. With two minutes left in the first quarter, the score was 18-10 in favor of the Falcons. John called his second time out of the quarter. He informed the boys that he wanted a full court press instituted and Thom would follow Chuck wherever he went on the floor. To some Hawks' fans pleasure, Thom held Mr. Burns to four points during the remaining time in the half, not letting the Falcon's guards get Chuck the ball. Bobby made three steals, which set George up for three buckets. Dale also shot lights-out, hitting five shots in a row. Jaden manage to chip in with six points, four points on free throws as result of shooting fouls made by Mr. Burns. The halftime score was 32-24 Hawks.

The Falcons slowly battled back. Mr. Burns found the bucket again and the Falcons didn't turn the ball over. The score at the end the third quarter was the Falcons 46 and the Hawks 44. During the fourth quarter, John continued the full court press and went back to double-teaming Chuck Burns if the Falcons penetrated the press. This time he had Timbo and Jaden do the double-teaming. Mr. Burns was held to four points. Dale got hot again in the fourth quarter. The Falcons tired and started turning the ball over. The Hawks were again successful at the free throw line late in the game, shooting seven out of eight. The final score was 66-54.

The thirteenth game was with Sometown. John started George, Jaden, Bo, Garry Maeder and Terry Cowens. While the Comets had some problems offensively during the first meeting, they now had players who could score. Miller Ward averaged 15 points per game. Benny Spencer, a freshman who'd been brought up to the varsity, was short on experience but not on talent. At 6'11" and 180 pounds, he was a pure shooter like Dale Richter.. The Comets had problems defensively against teams that had height advantages like the Hawks. Benny could shoot, but he had some problems getting positioned for rebounds even with his height. The main problem was his lack of bulk. At the four-minute mark of the first quarter, the Hawks led 12-8.

Terry Cowens was in the starting lineup because his great grandmother was attending the game from her nursing home. Terry was playing in Bobby's position. Terry caught the Comet guard being too casual with the basketball and stole it, taking it to the hoop full court and then immediately assisting with a pass to George after another steal.

His grandma almost jumped out of her wheelchair.

Benny Spencer hit three out of four shots. Jaden and Thom accounted for the other points for the Hawks. John inserted Timbo, Thom and Bobby into the game and left Jaden and Terry in. Bobby took over the point guard position.. Miller Ward and Benny Spencer both hit shots, but Jaden and Thom matched them in the remaining minutes of the first quarter. The score was 24-20 at this point in the game. George, Thom, Timbo, Bobby and Jaden began the second quarter together. The score at halftime was 38-28. During the second half, John ran in and out of the lineup of Timbo, George, Bobby, Thom and Dale. John wanted these five to play together without Jaden and Bo to see how they would do. The final score was 70-54.

*

A significant game was played on the night of March 19, 1966, in Cole Field House on the campus of The University of Maryland. Texas Western College defeated the University of Kentucky in the NCAA tournament final. What made it important was that the five players on the floor from Western were African American. This had never happened before because it had never before been allowed. There was much ado about it prior to the game. Leading up to the game, the team had many issues regarding race.

There were also issues after the game. For example, when they won, no one brought a ladder out for them to cut the net down. Nevil Shed hoisted Wille Worsley on his shoulders to cut the net down. It was also the custom to have the winning team appear on *The Ed Sullivan Show*, and this did not happen.

Bo Washington and Jaden Rose had taken verbal racial abuse from Roseville players and fans at the games they played during their whole high school career. Buck had been exposed to slurs, as well. Among the team members, there had been a number discussion over the years about how this abuse was getting old. Co-captains George Riley and Jaden Rose called for a meeting to be held at practice the day before the game on whether the team wished to play the game. Buck and John listened to different members' thoughts. Buck contributed for purpose of discussing the details of the 1966 Western Texas game. Buck and John said they could tell the Roseville team not to bother coming, but that would only give in to their inappropriate behavior and they were better men than that.

It was decided to play the game and have Bo and Jaden start. They would work them into the offense as much as possible and lead the team out of the locker room before the beginning of the game. After the first quarter, the score was 26-6. Bo and Jaden had both scored 10 points. By halftime the score was 52-18. Jaden had 22 points and Bo had 18. During the remaining portion of the game, John substituted different combination of players every three minutes, but not Bo or Jaden. The Hawks played very deliberately as usual when they were ahead.

The final score was 72-32. It appeared the Roseville fans and players got the message, as by midway through the third quarter, the fans from Roseville were very calm and quiet. All the members of the Roseville team shook hands with Jaden and Bo at the end of the game.

Game fifteen was with Carterville. The Carterville five had struggled much of the season, averaging 45 points per game, while only once reaching 60 points.

For whatever reason, they picked this night to find their shooting eye.

The match started well for Carterville. They jumped out to an early lead 10-4 with four minutes left in the first quarter. The Carterville center came out from the low post to grab the ball at the key turn and drill a shot twice. The forwards both hit shots from each corner. Then, the point guard hit a shot from downtown. Carterville finally missed a shot at the three-and-a-half minute mark. But they continued their hot streak the remaining portion of the half. The score was 32-26 at halftime. In the third quarter, the Hawks slowly cut into the lead, and after the third quarter the score was 50-49.

The Hawks quickly gained control of the of the game and blew it wide open, besting the Carterville five 29-13 in the final eight minutes on the court. They hit 10 out of 14 shots from the floor and nine out of 10 from the free throw line. Jaden and Thom dominated the defensive and offensive boards. Dale made six out of six shots from the corner. The final score was 78-63.

The Carterville coach said, "We stayed with them for a long time, but they outlasted us physically in the fourth quarter with their stamina, their bench strength and sharpshooter Dale Richter."

*

Al Higgins and Jake Boron were two 36-year-old officials. They'd been officiating together since they were twenty. They officiated junior varsity games for five years and then after they'd established themselves as respected officials, they graduated to varsity. They also worked football games and umpired baseball games. They had been excellent athletes themselves in high school at Perigan and were known for good sportsmanship.

Jake and Al were well-liked by fans, coaches and players. The television show *Starsky and Hutch* was popular in 1975 and Al Higgins looked like Paul Michael Glasser (Starsky), so the players called them Starsky and Hutch. They established with coaches that they would not *spray* during games, meaning making too many close calls. They said they believed if contact didn't affect the outcome of the contest, they wouldn't call a foul, but if one team or both teams got too aggressive, they'd start getting aggressive with the fouls.

They said, "When a team doesn't shoot well, there's additional rebounding, causing more contact with players and requiring us to watch more closely. When teams press, we'll watch for slapping. We'll always try to make sure we're in position to make the right call."

*

The sixteenth game was with Canfield Academy at Anytown. Al Higgins and Jake Boron were the referees. They were officials at many of the Hawks games. Mr. Cowens, the athletic director, had contracted with Al and Jake for a number of games for many years, including working football games and umpiring baseball games. Canfield had three young men who were 6'5", 6'6" and 6'7" so they could match up well with the Hawks front men.

The first half was physical, with both teams exchanging baskets. Both teams missed contested shots and blocked shots. The score was 25-25 at halftime. Jake and Al were standing near the timeline and in front of the Hawks' fans bleacher section watching both teams warm up during the break. Daniel Riley voiced his opinion a few times during the first half. He was siting three rows up from floor just behind Al and Jake. He raised his voice loud enough so they could hear him comment that they could have called a few more fouls on Canfield. Jake and Al knew Daniel well. They had purchased insurance policies from him and were a little surprised because Daniel would root for the team but not often question the officials.

Jake and Al just smiled at each other. Jake and Al went over and brought both coaches together, explaining to them that they had warned players from both teams to watch their hands, and if they continued to do so, they would start calling violations. The third quarter was less physical but still was tight defensively with block shots by both teams. The score at the end of the third quarter was 39-38 in favor of Canfield.

The score at the six-minute mark of the third quarter was tied 43-43. At this point, Dale Richter hit four shots in row from the corner. Jaden Rose went the hoop three times for buckets. Jaden and Thom controlled the defensive and offensive boards. George and Bobby also played restraining defense and they made four out of four free throws. The final score was 73-52.

At the end of the game, Daniel caught Al's and Jake's eye and mouthed *good game*. They just smiled.

The seventeenth game was with Brownsville at Brownsville. John started Jaden, Thom, Dale, Bobby and George. The Brownsville coach decided to double-team Dale. This worked for four minutes, as the score was 10-7 at that point. John called timeout and told George to set the offense up to get the ball to Jaden at any point on the offensive end of the floor. Jaden started hitting shots from different areas and when he could, would look for Thom for an open shot. The score was 32-20 at halftime in the Hawks favor.

The Brownsville coach took the double-team off Dale, but the Hawks offense and defense were too much for their opponents. Bobby caused a bunch of turnovers and made a number of steals, feeding players for fast break points. George hit double figures in scoring for the first time in a few games with 14 points. The final score was 70-34 Hawks.

*

The Saturday after this game a Valentine's day dance was held. It was sponsored by the senior class for their senior trip to Mackinac Island. Jake and Charles Decker told the class in their junior year that they would pay for half of the cost if they could find ways to pay for the other half.

The Saturday afternoon before the dance, the team, except for Dale and Terry, met over to Thom's folks' pole barn. George's uncle Don had given George four sets of boxing gloves and four headgears. Jake and Charles built a makeshift boxing ring. Chairs were set up for those who wished to watch the event. Among others, both of Thom's grandpas

Frank Baker and Jake Decker, George's great grandpa the car dealer Otto Schmidt, Everette Perkins, Ken Schmidt and his dad Leo, and Jack Gipson were present.

As they were waiting for the first competition, Frank said, "The old term for a boxing ring was a *square circle* because they call it a ring but it actually is a square or a rectangle."

Leo Schmidt replied, "That's interesting."

Jake said, "That's nothing new to Charles and me. We've heard Frank say that many times before at his butcher shop whenever we're discussing boxing."

Frank joked, "What did you say? I didn't hear you. I need to get new glasses."

Jake rolled his eyes and replied, "I've heard that one before, too."

They went back and forth like that for a short period of time before the matches. It was entertaining to the people around them to watch and hear the innocent banter.

The idea was to have the boys who participated go two minutes with headgear on. Daniel guided them a bit on proper technique. Everything was going well until the last match, when George wanted to know what it felt like to get hit without the headgear. After some consternation, Daniel relented. Bobby was George's opponent. Daniel told Bobby not overhit. This went okay until Bobby caught George near the eye. George's eye first turned red, and then two hours later it darkened.

Mary was going to wear a dress she and her mother had made from a pattern from Harper's Bazaar Magazine. She hadn't yet worn it because they'd finished it shortly before her mother got really sick, so it was going to be a somewhat special night in her mind.

Needless to say, when George showed up with a shiner, Mary was not happy at all.

She said, "Oh, isn't this just great. You and I are expected to have our picture taken for a yearbook section."

Her dad Jim had come in from working outside. He thought that it was a stitch and bantered, "Did you forget to duck? You should have had one of your buddies punch you in the other eye and you then you'd look like a racoon." Then he asked, "Must there be picture of you two in the yearbook?"

Mary answered, "Since I am editor of the yearbook, then yes. I would indeed like to have picture of us."

George remained mute, which ended any further communication. The car ride to the dance lacked any conversation other than when George went to open the car for Mary. She snapped, "I can open it myself."

As they were walking in, George said, "You look nice tonight in that dress."

Mary just said something undetectable under her breath.

Once they were in the dance, it didn't get any better, and the teasing still continued.

Buck, who was a chaperon with Jane Vogel and others asked, "What did you do piss off Mary?"

Mary went off with some friends, so George gathered with some of his buddies in the corner of the gym. Timbo said he was glad someone else was in the doghouse, because he appeared to be into it lately with Amelia for various reasons, including not spending enough time with her.

Jaden said, " I'm not in any doghouse with Sherlee. In fact, I'm in the penthouse. She says she loves me all the time." He continued, "Of course, she's busy with cheering and other such things in Sometown."

Thom said he was doing all right with Lisa Brooks. They spent a lot of time together on the school paper.

George said he and Mary had been doing all right until this happened. He said, "I hope she doesn't stay mad too long."

"Well, she came here with you, didn't she?" Thom observed. "So she can't be too mad."

George shook his head, stating, "She wouldn't miss this dance no matter what."

Thom smiled and said, "Well you two are made for each other. It'll all work out."

George went over and sat down on one the chairs that formed a square around the dance floor. For some time, he sat there alone. Then Mary finally came over and held his hand. She explained that it wasn't just the picture, but rather more about the dress. Even her dad did not even know about how she'd made a new dress. She said she was going to tell her dad about the dress when they were on the way to the dance, but then, he'd started joking around and if she'd told him then, he would have felt bad. She said she'd been upset with George until he'd told her she looked nice in her dress. Taking advantage of the moment to make things right, George leaned over and kissed her and said, "You do look nice in that dress."

Jill Riley talked Mary into putting some makeup on the eye and George and Mary had their picture taken after the dance.

The Valentine's day dance was a crossroads for Thom, Jaden, Bobby and Timbo. Soon after the dance, Timbo and Amelia stopped going together. Amelia had evidently met Miller Ward from Sometown after the last Hawks and Comets game through Sherlee Brown. Amelia was a cheerleader for the Hawks. She asked Sherlee about Mr. Miller when they had a pregame meeting and discussion period.

Amelia went out with Miller twice when Timbo was out with "the boys." Timbo commented to his friends that he was somewhat disappointed, but he and Amelia had sort lost something they'd had before.

After the dance, Jaden asked Sherlee to marry him. Sherlee had screamed and said yes.

Ken Schmidt spent some time at the dance talking to Amy Dotson, who'd come with Bo to the dance and who had broken her ankle skiing. Jade Rose was dancing with Bo Washington most of the night. Ken was getting around rather well with a cane but was not ready to shake a leg. Before the night was complete, they did an imaginary square dance and switched partners. Bo with Jade and Ken with Amy. Ken and Jade still remained friends for a long time.

After some discussion on the telephone with Theresa Williams on the Monday after Valentine's day, Bobby was informed that Theresa was now dating a fellow from college. Bobby moped around the school all day of the next game with Cotterville.

*

It was once again the same defensive dominance as the first game by both teams. The score was 6-4 after the first four minutes of the game. John pulled Bobby because of his sluggish play for most of the first half. John was concerned because Bobby wasn't playing his usual game. The game remained tight the rest of the first half. The score at the half was 23-20. John replaced Bobby with Timbo, who joined Jaden, Thom, Dale, and George. Thom and Jaden played heavy, attacking the defense against the low post players for Cotterville and causing them to make mistakes and turn over the ball. This created easy buckets for streaking Timbo and George. The score at the end of the third quarter was 43-30. The score with four minutes left the fourth quarter was 57-37. John and the coach from Cotterville started substituting at this point. The final score was 74-46.

The next day after this game, Bobby was still moping around school and at practice.

*

John and Gabby started an intermural basketball competition in December of 1975, every Monday and Wednesday night after the practices for the varsity and junior varsity during the basketball season. John and Gabby and sometimes Mr. Clausen oversaw it. Bobby ran the clock. The idea was to give the opportunity for those players who wanted to play basketball but didn't make the tryouts for the varsity or junior varsity to play.

The boys played six minutes per quarter. Gabby, Mr. Clausen, Buck and John arranged the teams based on their abilities 9th grade thru 12th grade. A schedule was provided for which team played which team. The games were played from 10 A.M. and 2 P.M. each Saturday. Kyle Schmidt played in this competition, and his team won the most games in the 1975-1976 year.

Because Bobby was still moping around at practice the day after the Cotterville and that night during and after practice before the intermural competition, John and Gabby took Bobby aside and discussed his efforts in the game and in classes.

After some discussion back and forth, John told him this was not the Bobby he knew who was always jovial and put his best effort forward.

Bobby said, "I know. I had the same discussion with my dad I'm sorry, coach. I'll try to get over it."

"Your first encounter with a breakup is hard," John said. "I understand."

The nineteenth game was with Nearbytown. Nearbytown season record was five wins and 14 losses. The Nearbytown coach Nick Jones had a dry sense of humor. He told the media that facing the Hawks was like David facing Goliath. He said, "Those boys from Anytown are a machine. Maybe I'll walk out on the floor before the game and wave a white flag. I'm proud of our boys, though. They work hard and don't give up."

John started Jaden, Thom, Dale, Bobby and George. They played five minutes at the beginning of each half and ran their different offenses. John wanted them to face competition not be stale for the next game. They also switched back and forth between a zone defense and man-to-man defense. For the remaining portion of the game, John substituted freely. The final score was 60-32.

The last game of the season was with the Morganville Wildcats. Morganville had an 18 win and one loss record. Their only loss was to a Class B school from Grand Rapids, Michigan. Morganville was located between Grand Rapids, Michigan and Kalamazoo, Michigan. They operated on speed, and they ran a full court press the entire game. Their coach mixed and matched eight players, placing them in and out of the game. It was a matchup of similar teams in regard to talent. John started Bobby, Thom, George, Timbo and Jaden. He felt this lineup would match up with the Wildcats' speed. George was very much capable breaking the Wildcats' press. The idea was to have Thom take the ball out, get it to George and depending on the situation, either have him break the press or use Bobby or Timbo as an outlet.

With a fast-paced offense, the Wildcats were ahead 18-17 at the end of the first quarter. Both the teams worked the ball around once they got past the timeline. Bob and Timbo shut down the fast break all but once. The Hawks didn't let the full court press cause any problems. It did slow them down. They were more deliberate with their offense, but so were the Wildcats. The Hawks edge ahead by halftime 31=30. John told the team he felt they had successful first half.

John sent in Dale for Thom for the second half. John had his eyes on getting a more substantial lead. Dale hit five out six shots. The shot he missed was rebounded by Jaden and put back for a bucket. The Wildcats didn't go away. They matched the score for score. The score at the end of the third quarter was 47-46 with the Hawks in the lead. The fourth quarter was more of the same with both teams trading baskets. The score with 10 seconds left in the quarter was 60-59 the Hawks' favor. The Wildcats fouled George. He made first of the one and one free throw. The Wildcats called timeout. George's second went in and out.

The Wildcat point guard dribbled past the timeline, passed it to his guard partner and his guard partner passed it back. The point guard took a shot from the key, and it found the bottom of the bucket. The overtime session continued to be a seesaw battle. With five seconds left, the Wildcats trailed the Hawks 71-70 after making a bucket. The Wildcats again fouled George. This time George made both free throws. The Wildcats had called timeout again between his shots. During that timeout, Buck and John told the Hawks to full court press but just create resistance not tight defense. The Wildcats never got a shot off. The final score was 73-70.

Jaden met a milestone that night. He surpassed Casey Adams's point total for a career of 1146 points. At the end of the night, Jaden had 1152 points.

*

Thom, Timbo, Bobby, Jaden, George and Dale were sitting together during their lunch period at *Jack's Place* the Monday before their game with Nearbytown in first game of the District basketball tournament.

George said, "Do you guys realize it's just 89 days until graduation? The time we have together is slipping away too quickly. High school will soon be over for us."

Bobby nodded. "You're right, George. This will be our last time together to hear the cheers and be the center of attention in this town for our basketball accomplishments."

Dale said, "Lads, let us therefore go forth and play our best."

"You bet, Dale," Jaden replied. "In my book we'll win it all. We certainly have the horses, don't y'all think?"

Jaden had committed to play basketball and baseball at Western Michigan University and was majoring in Business Administration. Bobby had committed to Ferris State College to play baseball, and he'd enrolled in their Pharmacy program. Timbo had committed the track program at Central Michigan University with intention having career in the medical field. Thom enrolled at the University of Michigan to study Dentistry.

George said he was going to commit to marrying Mary Klein and work for his dad selling insurance, as well as possibly working with her dad, Jim. When Charles told Jake and Frank that Thomas was going to go into Dentistry, they made a few wry comments.

Frank said to Thom, "I never thought you'd look down in the mouth."

Jake said, "a good Dentist is very picky when you have your teeth cleaned," Jake added, "but a great one never gets on your nerves."

Frank grinned. "Thomas, you're going to help people put their money where their mouth is."

*

Buck, John, Gabby and Jane Vogel started playing the card game euchre on Sunday afternoon in mid-January. Buck and John had watched the boys play it in school and on the bus and had learned the game. Gabby and Jane already knew how to play. John and Buck discussed game plans throughout the afternoon. Jane and Gabby carried on a lively discussion. All four talked more about random things than playing the game.

The Saturday morning prior to the first district game, the good old boys down at the barber shop were discussing how far the Hawks were going to go in this year's tournament. Most agreed they had the talent, but the talent would also level out the further they went in the competition.

The discussion the changed to Buck and Jane spending time together. Frank said, "They're billing and cooing. When the cooing is over, the billing comes."

Dave Sanborn said, "I'm still cooing. It's worth the billing."

"You know," Frank replied, "I wish I was still cooing with Emma. You're right, David. Of course, Emma did all of the billing in the butcher shop and paid all our bills."

Normally, John headed out at six in the morning to run the vending machine route. But this particular Tuesday morning was the morning before the first district basketball game at Anytown gym. John was helping his father-in-law with a broken pipe which had flooded the basement of *Jack's Place*. According to the weather report, it was going to snow any minute. John wasn't superstitious, but he felt it might be an omen for what the day was going to be like.

John and Jack Gipson finally got the water pipe fixed and most of the water removed by 11 A.M.

The vending machine business had taken off wonderfully; therefore, covering the route took some time. Dick Vogel, who usually ran the route on Saturdays and Sundays, was not available because he was in school, and Tony Ponza was already running the other route. The snow slowed down the travel, so getting to the sites took a little more time than usual. John found most of the machines at the locations were empty or close to being empty as result of morning snacks and lunch hour. Was this another omen?

*

The district tournament game between Nearbytown and Anytown started at 6 P.M. John arrived at the game at 6:45 P.M. Buck was very much capable of coaching the team, but John wanted to be at the game on time and be in the locker room before the game. The score was 32-23 at halftime.

The officials were calling the game very close. Buck thought sometimes they called close games when they felt one team, such as the Hawks, was greatly favored over the other.

Buck asked the officials, "Are you fellows going to call fouls close to the vest tonight?"

One official answered, "If it's foul, we're going to call it."

The other official nodded.

They indeed did call close fouls. George, Jade and Thom had three fouls each by halftime, while Bobby, Timbo and Bo had two fouls each. Dale and Banjo had one foul apiece. The game was close because of the free throw shots. The Nearbytown boys only made 11 out 26 free throws. Buck was given his first technical foul of his career when at halftime, he muttered to the officials in passing on the way to the locker room, "I guess you are calling them real close."

John and Buck informed the Hawks in the locker room that they should play good defense and not give into the opposing players. Four of the starting five plus Bo fouled out in the second half. The non-starters plus Dale finished the game.

The final score was 68-57 in the Hawks favor. Thirty-six fouls had been called on the Hawks. On the other hand, fourteen had been called on the Nearbytown players.

John said to Buck coming off the floor, "I knew this morning when I saw the snow and the broken pipe down at *Jacks Place* that they were bad omens. Then when I saw which officials we had I knew I was right."

John told the Hawks in the locker room, "We may have had a rough night, but I'm proud of the way you conducted yourselves. We won, which is good, but your sportsmanship made you a bigger winner."

Needless say, the Hawks fans weren't happy with the officials. Daniel Riley, Frank Baker, Jake Decker and others had yelled a few comments throughout the game. Even Everette Perkins had a few moments of verbal exchange with the officials.

The next day at the barber shop they discussed the game, among other things.

Sometown had defeated Cotterville 54-48 in the second game on Tuesday, so Sometown would play the Hawks on Thursday night in the second game after Perigan played Brownsville. Brownsville had drawn a bye in the first round while Perigan had defeated Canfield Academy 48-38.

The Brownsville and Perigan game was refereed by the same fellows who'd refereed Anytown's game in the district. The men called the game close as usual but not as many fouls and more equally between the teams. Brownsville came out on top 51-42.

The referees for the Anytown and Sometown game were Zeke Russel and Russ Page. Zeke had graduated from Anytown in 1964. That was the first year that coach Hyatt had coached at Anytown. That year, the Hawks had a record of 14 wins and five losses during the regular season.

They won the first two games of the district. On a beautiful evening in early March, the Hawks played Riverside at their gym, 15 miles from the Indiana border. The game was close the entire game. Anytown led 51-50 with eight seconds left in the game. The Riverside point guard brought the ball down the court and made two passes, and the Riverside forward turn and shot. The ball hit rim and bounce off.

End of game?

Wait a minute. The Hawks center jumped and touched the bottom of the net ever so slightly, goal tending, called the referee. Coach Hyatt questioned the call to no avail.

Riverside 52, Anytown 51.

The referee who made the call telephoned the Athletic Director at Anytown the following Monday and said he may have made the wrong call.

Too late.

*

Riverside went to the semifinals. In 1964, they'd lost Flint Saint Mathew, who'd won the State Championship. After that game, Zach made a vow a few weeks later that he'd become an official. Zeke's mom and dad owned the pharmacy in Anytown. Zeke worked the soda fountain during his high school days and was employed at the county road commission soon after graduating. He worked within a truck on the county roads spring, summer, autumn and winter. He married a girl from Nearbytown and had two children who attended school at Nearbytown. Zeke's wife Janet was a third-grade teacher at Nearbytown.

Russ Page, a probation officer for the county, had refereed basketball games for 27 years. He was Zeke's father-in-law. They'd refereed together for 11 years and were well respected. They also umpired baseball games.

Benny Spencer was in seventh grade at the time the Hawks beat the Comets in the 1975 district game. Ward Miller was a sophomore and the sixth man for the Comets that year. Fred Miller, Ward Miller's brother, had been brought up to varsity for the last two games was a 6'5" freshman. With these three above average players, the coach from Sometown felt his team might have a chance of beating the Hawks.

The Comets' coach gave them a fine oration about how back when the Hawks had come into the district game underdogs, the Comets were outplayed and outhustled by the Hawks. He asked, "Who remembers that game?"

Spencer piped up, "We all remember that game."

The coach said, "Then let us go get them."

The Comets did play hard. Spencer, Ward and Fred led the team with a number of baskets; however, Thom and Jaden controlled the boards and often put the ball in the hoop. Dale hit his customary shots and Timbo, George and Bobby ran the fast break to perfection. The final score was 76-56 in the Hawks' favor.

Russ Page was a senior official, having so many years of experience behind him, so, he and Zeke were contracted to do the last game of the district tournament. The other two officials who refereed games in this district had worked games for 12 years and 10 years. Russ had worked regional games with Zeke and quarterfinal games in the past and with his partner prior to Zeke, Earl Mathias, who now worked games with his son Joe.

Dale Richter never spoke up much before, during or after games. He just followed the directions of any coach he had. Prior to last district game, however, Dale said, "Pardon my mode of speech, but I'm sure glad those hard-handed referees aren't working our game. They seemed to have chips on their shoulders."

His teammates smiled a bit. George said, "That does it. If Dale thinks they were unethical then they must have been."

*

Dale was an altar boy in his early youth. He helped with the Christian Doctrine (Catholic Sunday School) in his junior and senior years for younger children at Saint Joseph's Catholic in Anytown. He belonged to a youth group for Catholic teenagers with George, Mary, Paula Price, Jill and June Riley, among others. Though usually a quiet young man, Dale was more vocal at meetings for this group and at other times for church functions. Dale always knelt down before a game and said a silent prayer thanking God for the gift he had for playing basketball. Aloud, he'd say to the team before they left the locker room, "May the gifts of God help us play this game the best we can." The team would then respond with a resounding *amen* in unison.

*

Brownsville boys and their coach knew the district final was going to be a battle. When two teams faced each other a third time in a season it could be interesting. Even if one team had won the first two games, the third time could be charm for the team who'd lost, because both teams then knew the others' weaknesses and strengths.

John and Buck decided to operate a fast-paced offense. They started Timbo, Jaden, Bobby, Jaden and Thom. Bo and Banjo were substituted at various portions of the first half. Dale entered the game briefly in the first half. The halftime score was 52-32 with the Hawks in the lead. John and Buck played Dale and the other members of the team during the second half. The score tightened once at the four-minute mark at 67-61, but the Hawks prevailed 78-65.

Jack's Place was again standing room only after the game. Sherry and Jack Gipson and Jane Vogel were busy until midnight. The Hawks had captured a third district title in a row.

*

The Sunday after the Saturday night district game, Paula Price asked her parents to attend the 8 A.M. mass at Saint Joseph's Catholic Church in Anytown. Normally, Paula, her brother Andrew and her parents went to the 10:30 A.M. mass. In fact, sometimes it was difficult to have Paula arise for the later mass. As they entered the church Paula insisted on sitting behind Dale and his family. As they left the church, Paula gave Dale a hug and congratulated him on the win. The mystery was solved Paula admitted on the way home she'd more than liked Dale for some time.

Paula's dad said, "Haven't you heard? Dale is going into the Seminary after graduation."

Her heart broken, Paula said, "Oh where have I been? I never heard that."

There was no further comments from Paula.

*

The teams in the Regional Tournament were: Roseville, Morganville, Riverside, Ambel, Porterville, Litchville, Colbyville and Anytown. Roseville drew a bye in their first game, then defeated Gaither Christian and then defeated Carterville in their district final. Roseville was to play Ambel at 6 P.M. on Monday. Litchville was to play Colbyville in the second game Monday. Anytown was to play Riverside at 6 P.M. on Tuesday. Morganville was to play Porterville in the second game on Tuesday.

The regional tournament was being held at Grand Valley State College in Anytown. Morganville, Ambel and Riverside were the favorites in the tournament . Anytown had record of 23 wins and zero losses, Morganville had 21 wins and two losses, Ambel had 22 wins and one loss and Riverside had 20 wins and three losses.

At Monday's practice, Dale was the first to say the Hawks might not need to play Roseville.

However, Dale said, "We should forgive all those who trespass against us. I once heard that people who are angry and unforgiven tend to suffer from anxiety and loneliness and become isolated."

George agreed. "I heard that once, too."

Bobby and Thom, who went the Methodist church in town, agreed they'd heard something like that in the same terms.

Jaden, who attended the Full Gospel Church, said, "Our pastor said to turn the other cheek, but that's hard for a black person nowadays."

Timbo smiled. "You fellows can be a pain in the butt sometimes, but I forgive you, for you know not what you do."

Ambel defeated Roseville 80-44. Litchville defeated Colbyville 68-56.

*

The brainstormers had met at *Jack's Place* on Monday morning because Everette at the barbershop was closed on Monday. They had all agreed that this regional was not going to be cakewalk for the Hawks.

On Tuesday, they met again with the coffee pot on at the barbershop. The predictions of the crew regarding the winners of the games on Monday night had been correct. Among other things, the crew agreed that Morganville would defeat Porterville and Anytown would of course win against Riverside, but they would have a challenge.

The game with the Riverside team was close. Neither team led by more than five points throughout the game. Jade and Thom made a basket and George made a free throw as they led 5-0 to start the game. Riverside came back and scored the next six points on two buckets and two free throws. Riverside matched up well with the Hawks as an accurate free throw shooting team. Dale hit a bucket from the corner, making it 7-6 in the Hawks' favor.

The two teams traded buckets from that point on until four minutes were left in the fourth quarter. The score at this point was 70-66 with the Hawks in the lead. The Riverside center hit a turn-around jump shot and was fouled by Thom. He made the free throw, bring it to 70-69 Hawks. George came down the floor and missed a shot. Riverside grabbed the rebound. The Riverside center made a hook shot, making it 71-70 Riverside. Another miss by Jaden and follow-up bucket by the point guard from Riverside, making it 73-70 Riverside.

Dale made shot from the corner and was fouled, making it a 73-73 tie ballgame. Jaden intercepted a pass down low to the Riverside center. John called timeout. Buck told Dale to shift out to the key. George or Bobby was to hit Dale at that point and Dale was to take the shot. Time back in, Dale moved to the key and George passed to Dale.

Bingo! Dale hit the shot. 75-73 the Hawks. With 55 seconds left in the game, Riverside called timeout. The Riverside point guard dribbled to the timeline, but the pass to the other guard missed its mark and there was a turnover.

The Hawks held the ball. Riverside fouled George with 20 seconds left in the game. The bonus for fouls was one away. They fouled Bobby this time. Bobby canned both free throws. The score with nine seconds left in the games was 77-73 with the Hawks leading. Riverside quickly brought the ball down. Their forward made a bucket with four seconds left in the game. 77-75 with the Hawks ahead. George was fouled with two seconds left. He made both free throws. The final score was 79-75 Hawks.

Morganville defeated Colbyville 80-52 in the second game.

*

The barber shop crew was made up of mostly retired men, and on Wednesday morning, they agreed that they didn't need more cardiac games like the one they'd witnessed Tuesday night.

Everette piped up and said, "There may be more, so we'd better get ready for the ride if they are going to go as far as we'd like them to."

After some discussion, the predictions were that Ambel would defeat Litchville, and of course Anytown would defeat Morganville. They felt it was going to be a close game.

When the team got back in town on Tuesday night after the Morganville and Colbyville game, , Buck and John met at John's house at 11 P.M. They were going to discuss a new manner of running the offense.

Gabby sat around for a minute and listened and then said, "I've got to get to bed and get my beauty sleep for me and our offspring. 6:30 A. M. comes awfully early."

Buck left about 1 A.M.

They both addressed and introduced the new plan at the Wednesday afternoon practice.

Buck said, "I know at the beginning of the season we told you to know the offense and defense backward and forward. Well we're going to do something different for the Morganville game.

We realize this change will take some doing, but you are good students and should catch on appropriately. At times, Jaden is going to play point guard and Dale is going play secondary guard, but neither Jaden nor Dale will be in at a guard position at the same time. George will be secondary guard. Thom will be at center when Jaden is point guard and Timbo will be at strongside forward. Timbo will play weakside forward when Dale goes to secondary guard. Jaden, George, Dale, Timbo and Thom will need to play longer without rest. Coach Richmond will put up one finger when we want Jaden to become point guard and two fingers when we want Dale to play secondary guard. We'll play you at your normal positions at times, as well. The idea is to immediately set up Jaden and Dale for shots at different points on the floor when we come down the floor with ball and create some confusion for the opposition. We'll probably only do this for the first half."

The practice lasted a little longer, but the boys seemed to catch on to the purpose of the change.

Jaden and Buck were talking on the way home from practice.

Jaden said, "I'm a little nervous about playing point guard. I haven't played that position since seventh grade and that wasn't that much."

"You've got to say I believe I can do this," Buck said. "You played the position well in practice."

"But Dad," Jaden said, "that was in practice. This is going to be against the very good Morganville team."

Buck said, "I believe in you, Jaden."

Jaden kept saying to himself all day in school, "I believe," to the point where it was getting to be laughable.

When some of the group was together, Timbo finally said, "I believe you be crazy."

Jaden laughed, the others laughed, and it seemed to break Jaden's nervousness.

The barber shop crew heard about the changes. The gossip mill had the community a little nervous about creating a different process against a team like Morganville. Frank Baker made a comment that Buck and John may have had a brain lapse. However, he said, "They got us this far undefeated with their coaching. We shall see."

During the first two minutes of the game, the Hawks players stayed at their standard positions. Both teams traded baskets at that point and the score was 6-6. Then John put up one finger and Jaden switched to point guard Timbo entered the game for Bobby and played weakside forward. During the next three minutes, Jaden hit three long-range shots, and George drove in for two baskets. Jaden and Thom dominated the defensive boards. The score at this point was 16-8. The Morganville coach called timeout. After the timeout, Dale went to secondary guard, George went to point guard, and Jaden went back to center. Dale hit two shots from the key and Timbo and George ran the fast break for a bucket by Timbo. The score was now 22-10. The Morganville coach again called timeout with a minute left in the quarter. After the timeout, Bobby came back in, and the Hawks played their standard positions. The score was 22-12 at the end of the first quarter.

In the second quarter, John put up one finger for one procession and two fingers the second procession. Once George brought the ball over the timeline, he did this the whole quarter. The Hawks were more deliberate in their play, attempting to set Jaden and Dale up for shots. Jaden drove to the glass a couple of times and scored and shot from outside and scored. Dale score from the outside. The process worked because the Morganville team was confused the entire half. Many fans on both teams appeared surprised. The score at halftime was 40-28.

The Morganville coach's wife, who was sitting a short distance from the team bench, asked what was going on.

The coach said, "I'm not sure, but we'd better correct it soon." In the locker room, the Morganville coach told the team, "We're better than this. We need to play our defense the way we always have and forget where their players are positioned." He showed them again on the blackboard the defensive strategies he had called for during the number of timeouts they'd taken in first half.

During the second half, the Hawks players played at their normal positions throughout the half. The 12-point deficient at halftime remained steady throughout the second half. The final score was the Hawks 66, Morganville 54.

Ambel defeated Litchville 70-48 in Thursday's second game.

A rematch of the prior year's regional final awaited. The crew's prediction came true.

A Friday afternoon 2 P.M. pep rally brought in attendance Daniel and June Riley, Scott and Camille La Rogue, Alice Clausen, Frank Baker and Gail Jenkins, Jake and Josephine Decker, Charles and Irene Decker and Dave and Connie Sanborn.

Frank Baker asked Buck and John before the rally what had guided them to go with the strategy for the Morganville game.

Buck said, "We wanted to catch them off guard. They scouted our players differently. Sometimes you get the bear and sometimes the bear gets you. This time we were confident we were going to get the bear. Their defense was set up to stop Jaden and Dale at their normal positions. We felt if we could change it up for a half, we'd bewilder them. It worked better than we expected because they really became confused for the whole half."

The cheerleaders and team pumped up the pep rally, although the students and other fans didn't need too much urging.

At the Friday afternoon practice, Buck and John spoke of the Ambel guards and their 6'7", 280-pound center.

John said, "Boys, we watched the Litchville vs. Ambel game. You guys saw how accurate their guards are at hitting their big center and how he moves to the glass well. We also know the two guards move to basket well and have always shot well from the perimeter. Our object is to guard the Big Guy with double team. Jaden and Thom will have this honor. George and Bobby will play man-to-man on their guards. That leaves Timbo to rove and guard their forwards, who are slow moving. We believe Timbo is quick enough to keep them in check; however, Jaden will cheat a bit if their forwards should cause problems for Timbo. We will run this defense for the first quarter and see how it goes. This places Dale on the bench. We'll lose some offensively with Dale not in there, but we believe in you five seniors."

The crew's opinions were that Litchville and Roseville didn't have the talent that Morganville and Riverside had, so Ambel might not be as hard to beat as the teams they'd already defeated.

Jake said, "Although we shouldn't think too much that way because we were favored last year and lost."

The field house at Grand Valley was packed. Players and fans from other schools in the Anytown area and in the regionals were in attendance.

Zeke Russel and Russ Page were set to referee the game. They'd refereed other games in regional but not the ones in which Anytown had participated. As game proceeded, it look as if the strategy was going to backfire. Jaden and Thom had two fouls on them covering the Big Man. John brought in Bo and Banjo to double-team him, but they also developed foul trouble. Banjo lacked height, but he had heart. Timbo was holding his own against the forwards and George and Bobby were also holding their own against the guards, although they scored three baskets apiece by driving and hitting from outside. The Big Guy was not a good free-throw shooter. He was nine for 16 from the line. The good news, if any was to be had, was the Big Man had only scored one basket.

The score at the end of the first quarter was 24-17 with Ambel in the lead. Bo, Jaden and Thom had two fouls on them, and Banjo had three fouls on him. John sent in Dale, Pat Simmons and Gary Maeder, with George and Bobby starting the second quarter. Timbo came in and out. The defense play was strictly man-to-man with no double-team on the Big Man. John and Buck did have Pat sag over when the Big Guy had the ball. Pat and Gary didn't have the offensive ability Jaden, Thom and Bo had but were above average defensive players.

Due to the accelerated defense by Bobby and George, Ambel's guards were reduced in their ability to get the ball to the Big Guy. In fact, Bobby stole the ball once, setting up a fast break basket to Timbo when he was in the game. He also stole the ball twice, setting up fast break baskets to George. Dale hit a few shots, and Pat took the Ambel forward who was guarding him to the hoop twice. The Ambel guards did score some from the outside and by driving to the basket. The Big Guy was basically shut down by Pat with two buckets. This was accomplished with only one foul by Pat. The combination of Pat's defense and George's and Bobby's ability to stop the Ambel guards from getting the ball to the Big Guy led to his scoring five points. The score at halftime was 38-35 with Ambel leading.

Buck and John decided to stay with the second quarter five in the third quarter. They explained to Thom and Jaden their reasons for continuing with Pat and Gary because of their success guarding the Big Guy.

Jaden said, "We are a team. We understand."

Thom nodded in agreement.

Buck explained to Bo, Jaden, and Thom that they were not using their usual athletic ability to guard the Big Guy. Buck said, "You fellows let him get you out of position."

Four minutes into the third quarter, the score was 45-43 with Ambel still in the lead. Dale hit three shots and Bobby drove to the glass. The Big Guy hit one out of two free throws and the guards hit three outside shots for Ambel. The five Hawks ran a straight man-to-man. Jaden and Thom entered the game, and they were told to play straight man-to-man defense.

At this point, the game took a turn. The Big Guy was called for two offensive charging fouls. He was also called for a defensive foul giving him four before the end of the quarter. The two offensive fouls were called on two back-to-back trips down the floor just before the end of the third quarter. Jaden, Thom and Dale scored on seven straight trips down the floor in the remaining portion of the third quarter.

The score was 57-49 at the end of the third quarter with Anytown in the lead. In the fourth quarter, the Hawks took control of the game. Bobby and George shut down the Ambel guards. John shuffled Pat, Gary, Thom, Timbo, Jaden, Dale and Bo in and out of the lineup. The final score was 77-58.

The Anytown Hawks were the regional champions.

Jack's Place was packed again, and *Joe's Bar* just down the street also had more than a measurable amount of clientele when the fans returned to Anytown from the game. Buck and John visited both locations for some time to share their joy with the fans. As usual, Buck was the leader of the celebration. John just stood back and enjoyed the celebration, speaking only when asked.

Sunny Bay was the team the Hawks were going to play in the quarter final game at Ferris State College, Big Rapids. Their record was 24 wins and two losses. They had defeated Shephard in the regional final 59-58. Shepard had been undefeated. Ken Schmidt, his dad and Ed Clausen scouted the game. They said they had two players up front that were 6'5" and two guards who liked to fast break. Their other forward was 5'10" but was excellent at getting in position for a rebound and could get off the floor just as high as players much taller than he was.

Ken said, "As Jaden would say, he has some jumps."

*

In Michigan, a number of areas had Maple Syrup Festivals. For many years, Jake, Josephine, Charles and Irene attended such a festival in Shephard, Michigan. The town and the area around it was a short distance from where Charles and Irene grew up. You could go on sugary tours to watch the process of developing the syrup from the sap. You also could go on rides on horse drawn wagons to see the method of tapping the trees, enjoy a pancake breakfast and place the liquid gold on the pancakes. There were vendors selling containers of maple syrup. There were rides for kids and adults and crafts from various talented people.

Josephine and Charles gained permission to tap the maple trees along the road by the golf course where they played golf. Scott La Rogue had a number of maple trees that ran along the road by his property. Jim Klein had some maple trees in a small tract of woods on his property. The window of time to collect the maple sap is weather dependent, requiring just the right temperature during night and day hours. The temperature can't be too cold or too hot or the season doesn't start. When temperatures rise to point that sap reaches the branches and leaves of trees, then the sap becomes skunky, and the season is over. The Sunday afternoon after the regional final, Charles, Jake, Jim, Daniel, Scott, George, Mary, Dale and Thom had a "bee" to tap the trees and install the service lines to the containers which would gather the sap.

When season was over, they had another " bee" to process the sap. Jim Klein had all the equipment to complete the operation. This had been a tradition for number of years. In fact, George knew much more about Mary over grade school, middle school and high school as result of the interactions with the Maple syrup "bees" than he did about Paula Price during years he went steady with her.

Whenever they'd start the syrup project, Frank Baker would say, "Look at the *Saps* working on that," although he had done sap tapping in his younger years.

*

Ed Clausen, Ken Schmidt and his dad Leo were at the Monday practice for the purpose of going over the scouting report. The scouting report from Ed Clausen showed that when Sunny Bay had played Shephard in the regional final, they'd played full court press the whole game. Ed said the Hawks might be able to score off the press if they tossed the ball over the press to Timbo, who would quickly surpass the defense because their safety valve was slow moving and Timbo could use his speed to the Hawks advantage. Normally, Bobby would take out the ball when there was a score, but George's ability as the quarterback on the football team would be an advantage to connect with Timbo. Many thought that if Timbo hadn't run cross country, he would have been an asset to the football team as a pass catcher. Timbo was also excellent at making breakaway baskets.

Ed and Leo said the Sunny Bay guards liked to run a fast, but one the guards wasn't real talented at handling the ball when bringing it down the court. After some discussion, it was agreed that the Hawks would run their own full court press, which would be a man-to-man press. Bobby would guard the guard in question.

John started Pat Simmons, Gary Maeder, Bobby, George and Timbo. The start of Pat and Gary was a reward for the Ambel game. The start of game saw Sunny Bay get the tip and going down and scoring. George took out the ball and hit a streaking Timbo for a basket. Bobby stole the ball from the guard after he dribbled twice and hit George for a bucket. Bobby again stole the ball and hit Pat for a basket. The Sunny Bay coach called timeout.

Thom and Jaden came into the game after the timeout. The Sunny Bay coach now had the 5'10" forward help bring the ball down. After a Bay score, George again hit Timbo for a basket. The connection after a basket by the Bay continued between George and Timbo for the entire first and second quarters. The fans from the Bay were yelling at their coach to take the press off. John took the Hawks press off at the end of the first quarter. The Bay guard went back to helping bring the ball down the court. The Bay five managed to score enough points to stay 12 points behind at halftime. The score at halftime was 40-28. Timbo had 20 points.

During the second half, the Bay took the press off. Pat and Gary started the second half with Dale, George and Bobby. The two teams traded baskets for three minutes. Gary scored one basket and two free throws. At this point, Jaden and Thom enter the lineup. The 5'10" forward began getting positions on the Hawks for rebounds. John was substituting Banjo, Timbo and Bo to keep everyone fresh. The Bay edged closer and closer throughout the remaining portion of the game but never made it closer than six points. The final score was 80-70. All of the points in the last two minutes were a result of the Hawks making eight out of eight free throws.

For years after the game, many Sunny Bay fans thought they'd have won the game if the coach would have taken the press off earlier.

The Hawks team was greeted at the outskirts of the town with a parade of cars and other vehicles. The celebration didn't last long because people had to work the next day, which was Thursday. Bobby had looked for Theresa Williams before and after the game but hadn't seen her.

*

The next opponent for the Hawks was Frankenmuth, who defeated Flint Saint Mathew 51-48.

Jake, Josephine, Irene, Charles, Thom and Rita had gone to the Frankenmuth Bavaria Festival in June of every year. Emma and Frank had also gone a few years. In June of 1976, Charles, Irene and Thom got a motel room in Frankenmuth. Thom met a young lady in the swimming pool whom he spent some time with. Her name was Karen Knight, and she was from Sandusky, Ohio. Thom and Karen had written back and forth. Karen had worked two years at the Cedar Point Amusement Park, first working in concessions and then taking tickets at the gate.

Thom had dated other girls, Lisa Brooks mostly, but wasn't really attached to anyone except Karen. Recently, Karen informed him she would also be attending the University of Michigan, majoring in Dental Hygiene.

*

Ed Clausen reported that Frankenmuth had only one young man over 6'. He was 6'2". The guards were 5'7' and 5'6" and the forwards were

5'11" and 5'10". However, Ed said they were a scrappy group. The front men were excellent at getting position for rebounds and could get above the rim very easily. The guards were just as quick as Timbo and Bobby. The front men clogged up the middle and didn't allow driving the ball or passing inside. They played zone defense and left open the outside shot to be made with their collapsing defense. Ed said Flint Saint Mathew tried to lob the ball into their taller players and their front men to rise up and intercept the ball. Ed said they tempted a team to shoot from outside. Their offense was very deliberate when they couldn't fast-break, Ed further reported. Saint Mathew stayed with their guards because they also had speed, but offensively they didn't have players who could shoot from the outer perimeters.

Thursday morning, the barbershop crew got wind of the Ed's report. They all agreed that the offense needed to work so Dale would be able to shoot more.

Pat Simmons's grandfather Mike said, "I guess we'll leave that up to Buck and John. They've done a great job of getting us this far with the boys.

During practice, Ed explained to the team what his report entailed. After his report to the team, the boys understood what they were in for.

Buck explained what was going happen. Jaden was going to play point guard. Bo was going to play center. Dale was going to play secondary guard. Bobby and Timbo were going to play forward on offense. Bobby and Timbo were supposed to guard the two back court men with man-to-man on defense. Jaden was going to guard the center and Bo and Dale would guard the forwards. Buck said, "We'll start the game in this manner and see how it goes."

The game would be played at Jenison Field House East Lansing at Michigan State University.

Buck told the team in the locker room before the game, "We are now in the semi-finals. Think back on all the work you fellows have done from the beginning of the season. That's why you're here today. All thirteen of you have worked as a team, and tonight we'll again work as a team. We deserve to win, so let's go out win this one."

The Hawks controlled the first quarter of the game. Jaden hit five out of six shots and Dale went six for six. The Hawks led 23-18 at the end of the quarter. The second quarter belonged to Frankenmuth. They ran the fast break against the Hawks very efficiently. They played deliberate defense when the Hawks had the ball on offense. They switched to man-to-man defense while still sagging in to stop the Hawks from driving to the basket. Jaden went one for four in shooting the ball and Dale shot zero for three. The score at halftime was 32-31 with Frankenmuth ahead.

John started Timbo, Jaden, Dale, Bobby and George to start the second half. Thom and Bo subbed in. The players returned to their normal positions. Dale hit it two shots from the side, but neither George nor Bobby could get the ball to Jaden, Timbo or Thom. The Frankenmuth front men sagged to stop any penetration or passes down low. The Frankenmuth front men also held their own on the boards. Bobby and George made one bucket apiece. The Frankenmuth front men had four put-backs on missed shots from the perimeter and their guards made two shots from outside. The score at the end third quarter was 44-38 with Frankenmuth in the lead.

John put in Bo, Jaden and Thom as the front men. John challenge them to take control of the boards. George and Bobby remained at the guard positions. Jaden became a force on the boards. The Hawks went ahead at the two-minute mark 52-50. Frankenmuth moved the ball around until the one-minute mark, when the 5'6" guard hit a jump shot, making it 52-52.

John called timeout. George brought the ball down and passed it to Jaden for an alley-oop at the thirty-second mark, making it 54-52. With ten seconds left, the Frankenmuth center popped out and hit a turn-around jump shot. The score was then 54-54. John called timeout and Dale entered the lineup. The play was set up for Dale to take the shot, but he was well guarded, so Bobby took the shot.

No dice! Overtime.

Both teams traded baskets in overtime. The Frankenmuth five were extremely deliberate on offense. Jaden didn't allow any defensive rebounds and had one put-back when Thom missed a shot. Dale made the other bucket. Time ran out on the first overtime without any more scoring. The score was tied 58-58. In the second overtime, the score was 62-62 with 25 seconds left. The 5'6" guard brought the ball over the timeline for Frankenmuth. He took his eye off the ball for just a moment when he looked left to pass the ball, and Bobby stole the ball and head for the bucket, making the lay-up. 64-62 Hawks with 18 seconds remaining. Frankenmuth called timeout. The guard was noticeable upset. Once again, the same guard came down with the ball past the timeline. Bobby guarded him closely. Once he crossed the line, he passed to the other guard, who hastily put up a shot that was off the mark with 12 seconds remaining. Jaden grabbed the rebound he passed the ball to George, who was fouled with nine seconds left.

Bobby walked up behind George and said, "End this right now."

George nodded and took the ball.

Swish. One point. He stared at the rim and shot one more point, making it 66-62. The same guard brought ball down and took a shot with four seconds left.

No dice for Frankenmuth.

Jaden grabbed the rebound and was fouled. He made both the free throws. The final score was 68-62. Jaden had 22 points, 17 rebounds and 11 assists.

John said to the media after the game, "We were so lucky to get out of here with a win. Frankenmuth was like all the teams we've played in the last few games. They were a tough opponent. We hung in there and won the game. I don't drink much, but I may have a couple of beers tonight with Ed Clausen and Buck Rose."

When he was interviewed, Buck commented, "Frankenmuth was a tough team, but we came out on top. All thirteen of these players have contributed in different ways. John and I have worked together well all season, but they're the reason we are here at this moment. However, we still have a date tomorrow at 1 P.M. for the whole marbles with Coppertown."

*

John and Buck and the Hawks had watched Coppertown defeated Littlefield 88-80.

After the game, Thom and his parents met up with Karen Knight and her parents. It was a surprise, as Karen hadn't told Thom that she and her parents were going to be at the game. Thom didn't know until after the game. Both families stayed at different motels in Lansing.

Karen asked, "We understand Thomas can't stay out too late as he has the big game tomorrow, but we can have dinner together?"

It was so cute that she called him Thomas.

*

Theresa Williams's uncle was the junior varsity coach at Coppertown. Theresa was at the game with a friend from Big Rapids, Judy Wesley. When Bobby was at the concession stand during halftime of the Coppertown and Littlefield game, she came up to talk to him and hugged him.

Bobby said a few words, but Theresa did most the talking. *Yup* and *nope* were mostly the words Bobby uttered. Then he finally said, "Well, see you later. Good luck to Coppertown. I hope we meet them in the finals.

Theresa said, "I guess he forgot about me," under her breath.

When Bobby got back to his seat with the team, he told George, "I just saw Theresa. I'm not sure what I ever saw in that gal."

*

Paula Price's sister was a sophomore at Michigan State University. She stayed overnight with her sister, as her parents had obtained a motel room. After the game, she suggested that her sister and parents have dinner with Dale and his parents.

A coach from Hope College saw Dale at dinner, so he came over to try to convince Dale to play basketball for Hope College. Dale told the coach, just as he'd told a number of other coaches who'd tried to recruit him, that he was going to enter the seminary.

Paula's dad told her, "You'd better give up on any connections between you and Dale."

Paula said, "Oh, Dad. We're just really close friends. We have been since first grade in Catholic Christian Development classes."

*

Copper is found almost exclusively in the western Upper Peninsula in the area known as the Copper Country. The copper in Copper Country is highly unusual among copper districts because it is predominantly found in form of pure copper metal (natural copper) rather than the copper oxides or copper sulfides that form copper ore at almost every other mine.

Coppertown was located in this area.

Jack Appleton was the coach of Coppertown. Jack's nickname was Mr. "Applejack. Dolly Parton had a song called Applejack, and he was nicknamed for the song.

Furthermore, Mr. Appleton played banjo, so his players would say, "Play a song for me, Mr. Applejack." There are Chippewa in the western portion of the Upper Peninsula and Jack was a Native American.

Jack was asked by the media from the Upper Peninsula some time before the game what he knew about the Hawks. He replied, "All I know is what we've seen in the last few games of the tournament. What we do know is they're a talented team who works hard and has good sportsmanship. These are the same traits my gentlemen have, so it should be an excellent match up. Both teams are unselfish in their movement of and sharing of the ball.

Lonny Barnes, the front man who'd broadcast several of the Hawks games, requested an interview with John regarding the Coppertown and Hawks game. John told Buck to handle it. He said, "You're much better at interviews."

Lonny was conducting the interview with other members of the media including the State Journal from Lansing. Buck's comments on both teams mirrored Coach Appleton's comments.

The Coppertown team liked to run and gun. They had a couple of games where they scored over 90 points and one game where they scored

102 points. They moved the ball around and all five players could score from their positions. There were two players who could enter the game and also hit the shot. They were excellent at handling the ball and didn't turn over. They had four 6'6" players who could rebound. Their only weakness if any, was they didn't play exceptional defense. They rely on their offense to win games. Many of their games found the opposing team staying with them in scoring.

John and Buck chose to run a full-court press using two different lineups of ten members of the team. The idea was to slow down their fast-pace offense by giving them resistance. Jaden, Pat Simmons, Dale, Bobby and George started the game, while Banjo, Bo, Thom, Timbo and Gary Maeder entered the game with three minutes gone in the in the first quarter.

John said to the players in the locker room prior to the game, "You've all contributed to where we are today and you'll all have another opportunity in your own way to contribute to this game. There's an idiom that says *virtue is its own reward*, which means that sometimes you don't get rewarded for what you do, but virtue or merit is in what you have done. You've already been rewarded for your hard work and sportsmanship each time you've won a game. You have one more opportunity to be rewarded, so let's go out and do our best to win this game."

The spirit before the game was magical. As the game began, it was evident that both teams were very emotional. The first three minutes remained scoreless until Jaden put back a missed shot for a bucket. Mr. Appleton called timeout and substituted. John sent in Banjo, Timbo, Thom, Bo and Gary Maeder. In the next three minutes, Coppertown scored eight points and the Hawks matched those points. The score at this point was 10-8 Hawks.

John called timeout this time an inserted the starting five. The Coppertown five didn't have trouble getting the ball down the court, but the press slowed them down from trying run their normal offense. The score at the end of the first quarter was 15-12 with the Hawks in the lead. Coppertown and the Hawks had both played in big games, but this game appeared to have grabbed both teams by the collar. The next three minutes provided two baskets for each team. The Hawks now led 21-16 because of Timbo's two free throws in addition to the Hawks' two buckets. At this point, John again made the switch to the second team.

Mr. Appleton also made some changes in subs and attacked the press. He told his players, "Once you get through the press, don't be afraid to put the ball up. We have the talent to get the rebound if we miss."

Coppertown scored 12 points from this time to the end of the quarter. John made a change back to the starters at the two-minute mark in the quarter. The two Hawks five also scored 12 points during this period of time. Banjo hit two shots and Timbo and Gary had two points apiece while they were in the game. Jaden and Dale had a bucket apiece while they were in the game. The score at halftime was 33-28 Hawks.

In the locker room, Mr. Appleton showed his team how they could tighten up their defense.

John and Buck mostly said, "We just need to keep playing our game like we always have."

John started Dale, Jaden, Thom, George and Bobby. The first two minutes of the second half began like the first three minutes of the first half. Both teams played a tight defense. Five trips down the floor for Coppertown provided no score, as did five trips for the Hawks. Both teams were very deliberate in their play. At this point, Mr. Appleton subbed in his two reserves. John went with Jaden, Bo, Timbo, Thom and George. The next three minutes saw Coppertown score eight points and the Hawks score four points. The score at this point was 37-36 with the Hawks still ahead. John subbed in Terry Cowens and Ed Newton. In the remaining two minutes, Terry made an uncontested layup because of an error on the Coppertown wingman. Ed hit a jumper, and Jaden made a turnaround shot. Coppertown scored one basket. The score was now 43-38 Hawks at the end of the third quarter. Starting the fourth quarter, Bo, Banjo, Bobby, Ed and Terry were the Hawks players on the floor. All five scored a bucket in the first three minutes of the quarter, Bobby and Terry on two free throws. Coppertown scored three baskets.

John called timeout. He told George, Thom, Timbo, Jaden, Bobby, and Dale, "You guys take us home. I'll be rotating you guys in and out for the remaining portion of the game."

For a split second he didn't move. The ball was in his hands, his grip firm yet soft. Thomas Decker loved this moment. He was shooting a one-and-one free throw. Just 30 seconds prior, he'd made a pass to Kyle Schmidt for a bucket. Kyle had made two points in the final game for the State Championship in Class C basketball. Thom had many wonderful experiences in his life, but he'd remember this his entire life. This was going erase the missed shot of another time.

Coach John had said, "Better times were coming."

The free throws split the net. The final score was Hawks 67, Coppertown 54. The seniors had fantasized about this a thousand times and now it was real.

After the game, Coach Appleton commented that the Anytown Hawks' tedious press defense took the Coppertown five out of their normal game. He said, "We couldn't set up our offense quickly enough to control the action. At time, my boys were confused. Mr. Rose and Mr. Richmond did an excellent job of coaching their team. I'm very proud of my boys. We didn't win final game, but we had the talent and work ethic to win it."

Buck met with the media and said, "Mr. Richmond and I gave our boys direction, and they worked and followed through. They never questioned their playing time. They all played for the good of the team. John and I knew this team was capable of winning the championship but didn't want to get ahead of ourselves each game. The chicken doesn't cackle until it lays the egg. We can now cackle."

*

The crew, Charlie Stone (Bobby's grandpop), Jake Decker, Harold Jones, Everette Perkins, Frank Baker, Jack Gipson and Elmer Johnson, sponsored an after-game dinner for the team, coaches and community. After the dinner, they all adjourned to *Jack's Place*. Daniel Riley even had a couple beers.

Frank Baker and others had asked Daniel several times in the past, "Why does an Irishman not have a cold one more often with us?"

Daniel would always smile and say, "I like iced tea more."

A gathering of the community was held the following Saturday afternoon after the state final to honor the team in the Anytown gym. Buck spoke for the most part. He cited each player for their contributions.

John said, "Buck, I thank you for who you are as friend and partner."

Buck agreed. "There's no greater friend for me than you, John."

Co-captains George and Jaden thanked the fans for their following the team. They both said having the fans at the games meant a lot. They presented two plaques to Buck and John, thanking them.

John and Buck received Co-Coaches of The Year for Class C. The school board voted to give Buck the same salary as John and listed John and Buck in the job description as Co-Head coaches. This remained as long as they coached at Anytown. Jaden and Dale received all-state first team honors. Thom received second team all-state honors.

*

The prom was held the last week in April. George and Mary went together. Paula Price went with Andy Moore, whom she had been going with for two weeks. Jaden and Sherlee attended. Bobby went with Jill Riley and Thom went with Jill's sister June Riley. Timbo went stag. There was a junior who was a very nice, shy girl and who had worked very hard on the prom. Her name was Linda Mac Alpine. Several girls cornered Dale to have him ask her to the prom.

Dale said, "Why, sure. I think Linda is very nice young lady."

Timbo and Dale shared the evening with her. Timbo said afterward he was available for dancing and other entertainment and Dale was available for knowledge and kindness.

Dale said, "You are also kind."

Timbo teased back, "Then you're saying I have no knowledge, Dale."

Dale said, "It was just a joke."

"I know," Timbo agreed, "but jokes are my forte."

Bobby said, "It's funnier because Dale said it and he's not always joking around."

*

The seniors had their play the first week in May. The highlight was when they got Timbo to run around a fake tree. The fake tree had been placed as to emulate a maple tree. The narrator,

Dale, read a poem about the maple tree, its branches, trunk and leaves. Timbo was told to run around the tree during the poem. Dale put a Shakespearean tone in his voice while reciting the poem.

The last line in the poem was, "And the sap is still running."

The top ten in the senior class were announced.

They were as follows:

Mary Klein, Jade Rose, Jaden Rose, Thomas Decker, Richard Vogel, Robert Stone, Dale Richter, Paula Price, Amber Johnson and Amelia Martin.

*

Bobby, Thom and Jaden had started baseball the Monday after the state final in basketball. Timbo was running track. George decided to work for Jim Klein in his fruit-growing business after school and on weekends. George had been the Hawks catcher his sophomore and junior years. Banjo and Kyle Schmidt therefore stepped in, sharing the Hawks' catching duties and third base duties. Banjo had a good year, batting 520. Kyle batted 450. They both threw out several runners. The team won 16 games and lost four games during the regular season. Two of the losses were while the seniors were at their trip to Mackinaw Island during the second week in May. Bobby Stone had three no hitters and had six games where he struck out 10 batters or more. Jaden's batting average was 540. Bobby's batting average was 480. Thom batted 470.

The Hawks lost to Beal City in the quarterfinals 2-0. The Beal City pitcher struck out 15 Hawks. An error in the eighth inning and a home run accounted for the Aggie's runs. Bobby was upset that he gave up the homer. Bobby had picked off 25 players in his career to this point, but his 26th attempted was called a baulk by the plate umpire. This unsettled Bobby. Coach Dave had to come out and talk to him and told him to forget it and get the next batter. The next batter hit the home run.

Bobby's grandpop Charlie Stone had given up a home run in a crucial situation when he was young, so he set out to talk to and comfort Bobby about the game. He said, "Everyone has had the same outcome of some sort before. You can't be perfect all the time."

Bobby listen carefully to his grandpop and valued what he said. When he was eight years old, he asked his grandpop how he knew so much.

"My boy," he said "through aging and reading books. Many answers are found in books."

Dale Richter was valedictorian of the senior class and Mary Klein was salutatorian. At graduation, Dale started his speech with, "The sands of the hourglass have run out on our time together, but we always have our memories." He then commented on the joyful times they'd had together from kindergarten to their days approaching graduation. He then mentioned several of those good times. He said, "The world shall step aside to let those pass who want to better themselves. I believe we all want to better ourselves."

He continued, "We learned from our years of education here the history of how the world exists. What the world is made up of. The geographical layout of the world. We learned how to communicate verbally and through the written word. We learned what numbers represent and many other facts."

In her speech, Mary Klein touched on the fact that, "Without education, we wouldn't have learned the value of our origins. Without our education, we wouldn't have adopted lifestyles and methods of personal, family and social interchanges. We've been encouraged by our teachers and parents to go forward and use what we've learned to further our education or seek other roads in our lives."

Dale and Mary then took turns reciting the pledges the class had made.

Dale: *May humor and laughter grace us all the days of our lives.*
Mary: *May we know the lighthearted freedom of a secure individual.*
Dale: *May we gaze at the wonders of the world.*
Mary: *May we care for and respect the fertile earth.*
Dale: *May we have the vision of what is important in our lives.*
Mary: *May we expect good surprises, accept defeat and realize our blessings.*
Dale: *May we be blessed with love from others.*
Mary: *May we occasionally enjoy the stillness but also enjoy the music in our lives.*

Bobby, his sister Carrie, his parents, Jane Vogel, Dick and Angie Vogel and many others attended Paula Price's graduation open house on a Saturday night the last week in June. The open house was from 5 P.M. to 10 P.M. Carrie and Angie were bored, so close to 8 P.M., they decide to play hide and seek. There were enough people in attendance that they could find places to hide. Along the way of hiding for a fifth time, Carrie discovered Paula and Andy Moore behind Paula's house kissing and talking. She went back to where Angie was counting off time before she went to seek Carrie.

Carrie said, "Come with me to see Angie." They watched Paula and Andy for an extended time, peeking around the corner of the house, until Timbo Clausen yelled from a distance away asking what they were doing.

The standard, "Oh, nothing," was their answer.

Timbo joked, "How do you know when you get done if you're doing nothing?"

Timbo never checked what they were doing. Immediately afterward, they went back to playing their game until their parents told them it was time to go home.

The following Monday, Dave Sanborn told Bobby at dinner that Paula had entered the convent to become a nun. Her parents had dropped her off at the Dominican Order headquarters in Grand Rapids, Michigan Monday morning. Paula had told friends that she spoke with Father Mathews at St. Joseph's on several occasions and talked to Dale Richter about it, also.

Carrie's eyes got big, but she didn't comment.

She never did say anything about what she and Angie saw. Angie kept quiet, as well.

Gerry Martin

CHAPTER THIRTEEN

25 YEARS
Fast Forward to 2002

A meeting was held in early March of 2002 for the purpose of developing the 25th class reunion for the 1977 class. The reunion was to be the Saturday prior to Labor Day.

Jaden Rose and Bo Washington were also scheduling a 25th anniversary reunion of the 1977 State Championship to held at halftime of the first Hawks home basketball game in December. Timbo Clausen, Mary Klein Riley, Jane Withers Jones and Amelia Martin Forbes were present at the meeting. Bobby Stone, president of the senior class, and Thom Decker, the treasurer of senior class of 1977, were also present.

Timbo came in and sat down. He said, "Well, this will have to be a BOBBY DAZZLER." He'd borrowed the term from an Andy Griffith episode where a character named Malcolm Merriweather made the same comment when he spoke of a special event in the show.

Mary Riley said, "Timbo, you never change."

Timbo grinned and said, "I yam what I yam, said Popeye the Sailorman."

After some discussion, it was agreed that a dinner would be provided by the Vintage Restaurant, which was now owned by Camille La Rogue, Scott La Rogue, Estelle Pullman Jenkins and Calvin Jenkins (Gail's Son). The meal was to be roast beef or chicken with a baked potato and green beans.

In November of 2001, a questionnaire was sent out to members of the class of 1977 for input regarding the gathering. It was suggested that Timothy Clausen be the Master of Ceremonies and a trivia game by played on the Class of '77 school days. The standard *who is who, who is what, who is where* and *what have you been doing* would be followed. Those who wanted to hang out after the dinner could adjourn to *Jack's Place*.

Jack's Place was now operated by Ben and Jimmy Richmond, Gabby's and John's sons. A notice was to be sent out for the time and date of the function by April 1ˢᵗ . They hung around a bit and spoke of old times than adjourned the meeting.

REWIND.......

GEORGE RILEY and Mary Klein were in boat on Clear Lake on a Sunday afternoon in May of 1978. Mary had caught a nice blue gill and George got down on one knee to take the fish off the hook.

Mary quipped, "While you're down there, why don't you officially propose?"

George grinned and said, "Okay, Mary. Will you marry me?"

Mary said yes, and they were married the last week of September in 1978.

*

Karen and Thomas had gone together through college. Karen graduated from the Dental Hygiene Program and was working with Doctor Carl Edwards in Toledo, Ohio. After Karen graduated from the program, she and Thomas had an on-again/off-again relationship. After Thomas completed his dentistry studies, he shared an office with Doctor Earl Townsend, who'd been a dentist in the Niles, Michigan area for several years. Doctor Townsend's dad had played baseball with Thomas's Granddad Jake. The family had been going to Doctor Earl for a long time. In fact, he was the reason Thomas went into dentistry. At this time in 1985, Karen left her job and joined Thomas at the Townsend Dentistry.

In November of 1988, Karen told Thomas she was moving back to Toledo and marrying Josh Benson, a man whom she'd grown up with and who lived in her neighborhood when they were both young. Karen was going to go back to work at Doctor Edward's office.

Thomas's Grandpa Jake had died in August of 1987 from complications from Alzheimer's disease. He had been diagnosed in 1983. Then in February of 1988, Thomas's Grandma Josephine died. Josephine had taken care of Jake until September of 1986 in their home before he was placed in an extended care facility. Jake went downhill quickly after entering the facility. Josephine had said a number of times during his illness that looking back, she and Jake should not have been so stubborn for a while during their marriage and not been apart.

Some said she passed away soon after Jake's death because she'd been worn out from taking care of him. Others said it was because she missed Jake. Even after he was placed in the facility, she visited him twice a day.

Thomas took the three occurrences hard.

Irene said, "I guess I can understand the loss of your grandparents, but regarding Karen, you two never really made a marriage commitment to each other. Maybe getting away would be good for you."

Thomas decided to take two weeks off from his practice in July of 1988 and visited Leslie Brown (Banjo) in London. Thomas and Karen had attended a few games when Western Michigan played Eastern Michigan or Toledo in football. Leslie Brown had played in the Western Michigan band. Leslie had spent two summers at Interlocken music camp in Michigan playing trumpet and flute.

In Leslie's senior year, Charles and Irene Decker had sponsored an exchange student. Her name was Anna Osborne, and she'd also played the flute. Leslie's family tree had British branches. Anna and Leslie became friends in their senior year.

After graduation, Anna returned to the United States. Her parents paid for her education at Western Michigan University, and she was also in the band. Richard Vogel attended Western Michigan to become a teacher. Buck Rose had married his mother Jane. Charles Decker had several scholarships which paid for his education. Richard and Leslie drove back and forth from their homes during Richard's sophomore year and Leslie's freshman year. Then they roomed together until Richard graduated. Richard obtained a position at Nearbytown as a High School social studies teacher. Thomas, Richard and Leslie hung out together when Thomas came home for a weekend. They went to Western's basketball games and watched Jaden Rose play.

A year after Leslie graduated from Western, he moved to England and married Anna Osborne. They lived in London. Leslie taught music at Bentley Woods High School and Anna taught music at Camden School for Girls. Anna had attended Camden for a time and then went to Bentley until eleventh grade when she came to America.

*

SHE SAW HIM as she was driving past his house. Thomas was pitching hay from a cart to the center of his corral for his horses. June Riley had heard he'd just returned from London, England. She'd also heard that he'd taken the trip to gather his thoughts.

She pulled into the driveway and got out of the car, yelling, "Hi, Thomas."

He called back, "Hi, June!"

As June walked over to the corral, Thomas started to button up his shirt. June smiled and said, "You don't need to button that up on my account."

June asked, "How was your trip to London?"

Thomas said, "Great. We took in all the sites and went to Liverpool around the area where the Beatles put their boots down. Anna, Leslie and Anna's parents were great hosts."

Thomas and Rita bought a fruit farm near Anytown and six riding horses with some money Jake and Josephine had left them. Rita and her husband Abel Perez watched over the farm while he was in London. Thomas asked June if she'd like to go out for a ride on the horses.

"Sure, I would," June replied enthusiastically.

They rode for some time and then came back and sat at his picnic table and talked.

June had attended the prom with Thomas but was aware of Karen because he often spoke of her. George had basically arranged the whole thing. Thomas had asked her to dance once at a club near the campus when she was attending Western for her marketing degree. She'd sold him a couple of insurance policies from her dad's agency.

Daniel now had two insurance agencies, one in Anytown and the other in Niles, Michigan. George and his dad worked in the one in Anytown and June work in the one Niles.

June had always had special feeling toward Thomas, but she figured he was out of her league because of his family's standing in the community. Then in 1986, she, George, her sister Jill and Thomas played in a golf outing for Alzheimer's. She rode in the golf cart with Thomas and they communicated well. They sat in the clubhouse for couple hours after the event and sipped on two drinks with Jill and George.

It was at this time she'd become aware of what a wonderful guy Thomas was. She'd known how goodhearted he was to others before, but she never knew what made him tick.

They chatted a little more after the ride. Thomas ask her before she left whether she would like to go out some time.

Of course she said yes.

This was the start of a relationship that ended in a marriage ceremony in the first week in June of 1990. Thomas said several times after they were married that probably he had it in the back of his mind to marry June all along and that was why he held off on marrying Karen. Karen had asked Thomas several times when they'd get married, but he always had one reason or another for it not being the right time yet.

Karen visited his office a few months after they were married. She said, "I wasn't surprised when I was told by Leslie and Richard that June always spoke to you between junior varsity and varsity games after she finished cheerleading the first game and you were warming up."

Thomas said, "That may be true, but it was nothing more than a *hi, how are you.* June was rather shy in those days. Anytime we saw each other during our high school days that was about all the conversation that passed between us."

Four children were born to Thomas and June: Jacob in 1991, Josephine in 1991, Kathleen in 1995 and Daniel in 2001.

CARRIE SANBORN had grown to be 6'2". She was the Hawks center, and Angie Vogel was the point guard for the 1985/86 and 1986/87 women's team. Bobby Stone was the women's junior varsity coach with Helen Baer Sanborn as his assistant. Bo Washington was the varsity coach with Gabby Richmond as his assistant. Buck Rose was now Athletic Director and coached the football team.

Carrie was an excellent athlete. She played basketball, volleyball and softball. She was the pitcher on the softball team and Angie was the catcher. Carrie was most valuable player for all three sports. All the teams she played on accomplished an over 500% winning season. They won their district championship in basketball the two years she played and won their district in softball the three years she played that sport.

Angie Vogel was a good point guard. She could handle the ball and was a great defense player but had some problems at the free throw line. She was left-handed. Buck and her coaches tried to work with her, but she always had a low percentage in this process. She was fouled a lot, so they could have used her free throws. Angie was also a very good at track, especially in hurdles.

When he could, Thomas would attend Angie's sports events with Richard.

Dave resign from coaching baseball during the years Carrie played sports so he could be at her games watching her play. Though he didn't go back to coaching until after Bobby finished playing college ball at Ferris State College and Carrie graduated, he helped out at times when asked.

*

DALE RICHTER spent two years in the Seminary and then changed his mind about becoming a priest. He decided it wasn't his calling.

He moved back home and decided he wanted to become a lawyer. He entered Michigan State University in September of 1979.

There was a commotion at the hostess's area of *Mickey's Irish Pub* in East Lansing, Michigan. Maureen Kelly was raising her voice to the hostess. "For the third time, I told you we have reservations for three! I believe the gentleman is sitting right over there who will be with us. This is his sister. She operates a restaurant and doesn't treat people this way."

The hostess replied, "What is the name again, please? I just got here a minute ago."

"Maureen Kelly," Maureen said.

"Oh here it is." The hostess suddenly found the name

Maureen had finished high school when she was sixteen. She'd met Estelle La Rogue when she attended Ferris State College. She obtained a pharmacy degree and had been working in Battle Creek, Michigan at *Sweeney's Pharmacy*.

Dale was in his senior year at M.S.U. Dale had met Maureen twice in the past. She was very outgoing and said what was on her mind most of the time. Estelle said one time in jest that Maureen would invite people to party at her house and have a keg of beer and lock all the bathrooms if problems arose.

Maureen said, "I'd never do that. Then they'd have to pee outside, and that would cause even more problems."

Maureen sat down and said to Dale, "That lady got my Irish up. Sorry, my boy. I probably should have had more patience."

Dale laughed and said, "I was about to try to rescue you ladies if she'd asked you one more time."

"Estelle has told me you're rather laid back guy" Maureen said. "Ad that you think faster than you move. Don't get me wrong. I like guys like you."

Dale, Estelle and Maureen had a nice chat back and forth for a while. Maureen then asked Dale why he'd left the Seminary. Dale said, " I can't put it into words, but after a while, I just didn't think it was for me. I'm still a devout Catholic."

"Do you think you'll ever get married?" Maureen asked.

He said, "Possibly, in time. A man thinks he is incomplete and then he gets married and he's finished."

"That's really funny," Maureen said. "So you think marriage isn't a great institution."

He rolled his eyes. "It was just a joke, Maureen."

From that day forward, Maureen visited him every weekend when she could.

Maureen's dad was a pharmacist in Redford, Michigan. Her mother was a principal at Redford Union High School. Maureen was an only child.

Dale and Maureen were married in the first week in June of 1983, after Dale graduated from M.S.U. Dale entered Cooley Law School in the Lansing, Michigan area during the autumn of 1983. Dale's folks had a life insurance policy which paid Dale after their death and a savings account which Camille and Scott never used. They'd placed the money in a trust for Dale's college education. They intended provide it to him when he completed his studies for the priesthood.

The trust, Maureen and her parents provided funds for Dale's law studies. He had an apartment in the Lansing area and joined Maureen at their apartment on weekends when he could. Dale told friends that when he got to their apartment on Friday nights, it was late and he was so tired he couldn't turn the light out in the bedroom, so he usually waited until Saturday afternoon to arrive at their apartment. He said it felt like more of a visit.

Dale's and Maureen's relationship was intellectual and sometimes platonic. They shared thoughts and liked to discuss issues. They respected each other's intellect. Maureen told friends that she and Dale liked each other very much but you might not call it love in the first degree during their first three years of marriage.

Dale completed his law studies in 1986. He obtained a position with *Branston and Branston Law Firm* in Cheboygan, Michigan. George and Abraham Branston were Maureen's uncles on her mother's side. Maureen obtained a position as a pharmacist at *Clifton's Pharmacy* in Cheboygan a few months after Dale started at his law office. He became a prosecuting attorney in Cheboygan County in 1990 and became a District Court Judge in Cheboygan County in 1994.

In 1988, Dale met with Jaden Rose, George Riley and Timothy Clausen in Mt. Pleasant, Michigan at a restaurant called *Schmidtiwagen's*, owned by Ken Schmidt and his wife Jean Wagner Schmidt.

They talked a little and then Dale announced, "I'm going to be a father."

Timothy quipped, "Does Maureen know?"

"Very funny Timbo," Dale said with a groan.

George grinned. "Must be you got past talking high-brow stuff."

"Give him a break, guys," Jaden said.

Dale said, "Maureen and I found a love potion on the dresser in late 1987, I guess."

"I still can't quite believe it," Timothy said. "Dale is now a lawyer. Maureen told Estelle that you're an excellent one and have no problems representing your clients with verbal efficiency."

Dale and Maureen had four children" Patricia born on September 22, 1988, Carl on March 8, 1990, Scott on June 8, 1991 and Camille on December 19, 1992.

*

ROBERT STONE decided after one year at Ferris State College that baseball and the pharmacy program didn't mix. He decided to transfer into a general education program which at some colleges at the time was known as a liberal arts program. He thought maybe he would get back into the program at a later date. After his second year, he decided to enroll in the physical therapy program to work with athletes. He also convinced Timothy Clausen to transfer to Ferris and into the program because he felt Ferris had an excellent program. Tim tinkered with attempting to get some financial assistance through the college's sports program, but there wasn't any available for track. He lost his scholarship at Central Michigan, but he felt it was important to attend a school that had excellent program and he'd always had it in the back of his mind to become a therapist after attending therapy sessions with his dad after his dad's accident.

Tim still had the other scholarships he'd obtained for his further education. He and Robert found a downstairs apartment of a house which had another apartment in lower level and two in the upper level. The owner lived in Grand Rapids, Michigan, so he hired the two fellows to watch over all four apartments and perform any maintenance as needed. A garage in the back of the house was converted into a workshop for any tools they need for maintenance. They were given their rent free for the performance of the maintenance tasks.

Robert saw Theresa Williams on a number of occasions in his first year and she hinted about her and Robert dating again.

Finally, he said, "You aren't somebody I need in my life."

After that, they just said, "Hi," in passing.

Robert dated a number of ladies during his first three years of college, but most of the time he concentrated on baseball and his studies. During the first two years, he spent most of his time hanging out with his catcher Ernie Forten.

Dave Sanborn's dad had been a catcher in his day, so he really enjoyed baseball. He'd attended all of Bobby's sports events. Abe was a man who kept to himself most of the time. He sat with Dave at football and basketball games. He talked Bobby's grandma Sophia into going to home baseball games with him. He didn't spend much time with Bobby until Bobby's freshman year in high school.

Abe retired from the Army in 1966 after his son Donald died. Sophia took Donald's death hard. She wouldn't go out of the house very often for about two years. Abe never left her alone for too long. Then in 1968, she started spending time with some of the ladies around Anytown shopping, playing the dice game Bunko, playing cards and crocheting with them. She did not, however, have much interest in sporting events. She did go the semi-final and final basketball games in 1977.

Sophia and Abe went to all of Carrie's sports events, as by now they had rekindled their friendship with the community twofold and Sophia was now more outgoing, like she had been before her son's death. Abe started working with Charlie Stone doing carpentry work when Sophia started spending time with her ladies. Dave, Abe and Charlie went to Bobby's college games when they could, whenever he played at Ferris or Grand Valley State in Allendale, Michigan.

Mollie Stewart came to a baseball game at Ferris when the Bulldogs played Northwood College in Midland, Michigan, in the spring of 1980. Her brother Roy was playing for Northwood.

Robert pitched an excellent game, which Ferris won 4-1. After the game, Bobby took a shower and got dressed. Mollie spent a little while talking to her brother. Then she waited for Bobby to come out of the complex. She said she lived just two blocks down from where he lived and asked him whether he minded walking with her back to both of their living quarters. Their apartments were a short distance from the Ferris State Campus.

They chatted for a time in general, and then they discussed their majors. Robert told of his history regarding education at Ferris. Mollie told him she was in the environmental health program as one of the first women in the program. It was a program that readied students for protection of public health through inspections, proper construction of facilities and testing of products.

She asked him if he dated much.

He answered, "Not much in the last year. I've been concentrating on my studies and baseball. When I do something with other people, it's usually with Timothy Clausen, Ernie Forton or friends from my hometown."

She asked him if he'd like to go to a movie. *Private Benjamin* was showing at the movie theater in downtown Big Rapids, which was three blocks from Robert's apartment.

He said, "Sounds good. I need to spend some time with the opposite sex. Maybe this Saturday night."

Saturday morning, he called Mollie and told her his coach wanted him to go down to Allendale with all pitchers and catchers on the team and watch a double hitter game between Grand Valley State College and Hillsdale College. He said, "I don't think I'll be back in time for the movie. Timothy is free. He can take you."

She said, "Well, okay. That might be nice."

Timbo had already told Bobby that he knew who she was. He'd seen her in the hallways of the Health, Science and Arts building, as both programs for environmental Health and physical therapy studies were in this building. Timbo told him, "That lady is a looker."

Bobby said, "Well, you have my blessing."

"I thank you, Reverend Stone," Timbo replied with a smirk.

Timothy walked down to Mollie's apartment and then they walked to the show. After the movie was over, they stopped in a sub sandwich shop next door to the theater. They spent approximately two-and-a-half hours getting to know each other. When Timothy returned to their apartment, Bobby was back from Allendale.

Timbo said, "As Gomer Pyle would say, 'She's nice. Real nice.' I find her very well versed in many things, and yet she is not conceited. She's very down to earth."

"She probably is down earth," Bobby remarked. "She's interested in protecting the environment and the Earth."

Timbo said, "You probably know she graduated from Bay City All Saints in Bay City, Michigan."

"I did not know that," Bobby said, shaking his head. "When we walked back from the game, we just talked generally about our majors and few other things."

Timbo said, "Well, she told me that her brother graduated from her program in 1975 and worked at the Saginaw County Health Department. She said he enjoyed his work. Her sister graduated Ferris in 1978 from the nursing program."

Bobby nodded. "She did tell me that."

Mollie's family was French, English and German in ancestry. Mollie said her dad told her ancestors were renowned. She said, "Although, when we asked him the how, when and why he said, 'I really don't know.'"

Timothy said, "She mentioned the two of us. She said, 'I see why you and Robert hang out together. You have the same sense of humor. My father is the same as you two with his unusual quips.'"

Timbo said to Bobby, "I think maybe if she wants, I can be her steady Eddie."

As Timothy and Mollie were out walking one day, a funeral procession of cars came by. She noticed one of the people in the cars was a professor from Ferris. She asked, "I wonder who died?"

Timbo said, "I'd say probably the man in the first car."

"Oh, Timothy," she exclaimed. "You're really funny." She always called him Timothy. She told Timbo, "We always call my dad Poppa, but we never call my mother anything but mother. She will tell you not to if you call her anything else."

Mollie and Timbo spent time together until the end of the term in first week in June, when Mollie went back to Bay City for the summer. When her parents came to pick her up to go home, she introduced her parents to Timothy.

Timbo said, "I'm glad to meet you, Mollie's Poppa and Momma."

Mrs. Stewart looked down her nose at him but didn't say anything.

Poppa Stewart chuckled and said, "Nice meeting you, Timothy."

They talked bit. Mollie's mother didn't contribute too much to the conversation but remained quiet. Soon afterward, Timbo gave Mollie a peck on the cheek, and she left.

Mollie's mother again gave Tim a stern look.

Bobby and Timbo stayed in their apartment for the summer. They couldn't give up their good deal on the apartment. There was a married couple who lived in the lower back apartment of the apartment house who also stayed for the summer. The man was in the pharmacy program.

Bobby took a job at a convenience store. It was decided that one of them would watch over the apartments in case something needed to be done or repaired and the other would get a job. The one who got a job first would go to work. Timbo came up with this plan, but Bobby found the job first.

Bobby told his dad that he thought Timbo didn't try too hard to find employment. Bobby said, "Dad, we never were concerned when I was away at ballgames or when we were in class and such. I think it was a con job Timbo thought up. The truth is, I'd rather be working than hanging around the house all day."

After a few weeks, Timbo told Bobby that maybe he should have tried a little harder to find a job.

He was getting bored sitting around.

*

Angus MacGee, the first baseman for Ferris baseball team, was from Big Rapids. Angus was an outstanding hitter. Angus, Bobby, Timbo and Jenny Wilson hung out all summer playing partners in cribbage, euchre, and spades card games.

Jenny was enrolled at Ferris to work toward becoming a truck and other heavy equipment mechanic. She intended to working on large vehicles at her uncle's trucking business in Weidman, Michigan. After she completed her requirements for that certification, she decided to follow up with a program available at Ferris for teaching others who wished become a mechanic.

Angus and Jenny were in the same program. Angus's girlfriend was away going to college at Michigan Tech in the Upper Peninsula of Michigan. She was also from Big Rapids. Angus and Jenny said Theresa Williams was kind of a changeable person. She went from one boyfriend to the next in high school.

Jenny said, "Bobby, she's changed her major in college about as many times as she changes her hairstyle."

Bobby and Timbo purchased a car together. The car was in Bobby's dad's name and Bobby's name. Timbo and Bobby traded off making payments every other month.

Tim and Mollie wrote back and forth until the last week in July. Timbo would call her once a week from a pay phone just down the street. A phone conversation the last week in July went sour when Mollie mentioned that he never came down to see her but he would go home to see his parents and go other places.

Timbo countered, "Mollie, I went home once and went up to Ludington with Angus to visit his sister. That is it."

"That's okay," Mollie huffed. "The other night Marty, my old boyfriend from high school, asked me to go out."

Timbo said, "Have fun," and hung up.

When he got back to the apartment, Timbo told Bobby what had just occurred.

"Maybe you ought to go see her," Bobby suggested. "You probably should have gone to see her before this."

Timbo said, "Probably. I should have gone before, but she doesn't need to threaten me or whatever with an old boyfriend. She can find a nice day and go fly a kite." Tim shrugged. "You win some, you lose some and some are rained out."

*

When Mollie returned to school, she and another girl from her program started living in an apartment about a half mile from campus. On the third day after her return, she borrowed her roommate's car and went to looked up Timothy. She knocked on the door, but Timothy wasn't at his apartment. Bobby told Mollie that he was down at the Student Center having a drink with Angus Magee. She walked down to the Student Center. She walked over to where he was sitting in the food and drink court and sat down.

She said, "Well, you horse's ass, how are you doing?"

"Mighty fine," Timbo replied. "How are you?"

"I am good. By the way, I never went out with my old boyfriend," Mollie said. "Actually, I had a good summer working at my Poppa's jewelry store and hanging out with my friend Ellen Connors.

Timbo said, "You told me that before when we talked on the phone."

Mollie shrugged. "My old boyfriend did ask me out, but I told him I was in love with you. I told you I might go out with him because I missed you and wanted to get a rise out of you. Then you pissed me off because you acted as if you didn't care."

Timbo said, "Well, Mollie, I guess I really should have visited you prior to our phone call and probably should have visited you after the call, but pride and stubbornness sometimes gets in the way for me. I love you, too."

Angus said, "Sounds like it would be a good idea for you two characters to get married."

Timothy said, " Angus, I might just ask her to do that, but not here. Mollie, how would you like to go out to dinner tonight at a nice restaurant here in town?

"I sure would," Mollie said eagerly, "but if you ask me and if I say yes, you're going have make some amends for calling my mother *Momma*."

"I was only kidding," Timbo said. "I'm sorry Mollie."

Mollie said, "I told Mother that you liked to kid around, and she should be aware of it, since she lives with my dad."

Before he and Mollie went out that night, he called Mollie's mother and explained that he was sorry he'd called her by the wrong name. He told her, "This very night I'm going to ask Mollie to marry me."

Mollie's mother said, "The joke's on you, my boy. I don't care if you call me Mom, Mamma, Mommy, Mother, Carol or Mrs. Stewart. Mollie pulls that on everyone. You're just the first person who has actually called me something else when they heard her story. I decided to look upset because I knew what she'd done. She is evidently still trying to push your buttons. A day never went by this summer when she didn't speak of her love for you. She thought she might have gone too far with boyfriend deal. I understand from what she has told me that your morals are wonderful, you are very intelligent person, and you enjoy life. She says your sense of humor is like her dad's. You should have figured it out when her dad chuckled when you called me Momma."

"Okay I understand now," Timothy said, "but I still feel, thinking back, I know I shouldn't have called you that. I was just trying to be funny and wasn't thinking correctly. In truth, I'd forgotten what Mollie told me. I know that may be hard to believe, but I really didn't catch on until she told me today that you were still upset."

Mrs. Stewart said, "Well, Timothy, you have Mollie's dad's and my blessings. I think she'll agree to marry you."

Timothy said, "Thank you, Mrs. Stewart."

That night when he picked up Mollie, he shook his head. "You're really funny."

Mollie said, "What?"

"I called your mother a little while ago," Timothy said.

"Uh-oh. I've been had," Mollie said with a snicker.

*

Timothy had to take a few classes in the summer of 1981 to complete his studies, and Mollie also had to take a block of classes to complete her studies that had been created in the Summer of 1972 for the Environmental Health program.

The happy couple were married the last week in September of 1981. Ellen Connors was Mollie's maid of honor and Robert was Timothy's best man. They were married at Bay City All Saints Church. Mollie's uncle, Father James O'Brien, conducted the ceremony. Father James was Mollie's mother's brother.

Father Jim said to Timothy when he first met him for the instruction required before marriage, "So Mollie's Momma has okayed this marriage?"

Timothy replied, " Father, I think sometimes I have met my match with Mollie's family regarding humor."

Mollie admitted to Timothy a couple of weeks after they were married that walking home with Robert was a ploy to find a way to be properly introduced to him.

Timothy said, "You couldn't have just said something to me in the hallways at school?"

She laughed and replied, "I was going to, but when I was at my brother's game and Robert's, I decided it was an opportunity to be coy about meeting you."

"How did you plan to meet up with me if Bobby wouldn't have had to go to that double hitter?" Timothy asked.

Mollie said, "Robert asking me out was never in my plan. I was going to ask him to introduce me to you. I didn't have a real plan after that, other than as you said, take it upon myself to approach you. The double hitter worked that out for me just grand."

*

Timothy obtained a job with a firm who provided physical therapy for athletes in the Kalamazoo area. Mollie took a job at the local health department where Anytown was located. Both found the positions prior to graduation.

They postponed their honeymoon until June of 1982 because time off for vacation at both of their workplaces didn't start until they were employed for six months. They spent five days at Mackinaw Island.

They had a daughter Tammy born in January of 1983 and a son Lee Patrick born in of December 1985.

One day early in January 1981, Mollie said to Timothy, "Robert doesn't date much, does he? From what I have seen, a girl has to get know him very well before he will even talk to her more. Then he will say hi and not much more."

Timothy said, "Well, he never was one to be too comfortable talking to women. He really liked Theresa Williams because she was outgoing. This worked for him because could feel comfortable. Then she showed her true colors and hurt him, so he has been guarded ever since. In addition, he has said he needs to concentrate on his studies and keeping in shape for baseball. He told me I was smarter than him. He said I needed my tutor sitting beside me to take my S.A.T.'s. I told him he was full of bologna."

*

It was mid-February of 1981 when she rushed into the Student Center. Bobby was sitting by himself having some French fries and a Coke. For a week Jenny had seen him at the library, at different hangouts for college students, at the grocery store, with his baseball teammates and once with Tim and Mollie.

She wanted catch him alone.

She sat down she asked, "Can we talk?"

Bobby said, "Why sure, Jenny. What's up?"

"I need to visit my uncle in Weidman, Michigan on Saturday, I borrowed some tools from him and need to return them. I usually take some back roads there because it's shortcut, but those roads are snowy this time of year, so I'd like a companion to go with me."

"Okay," Bobby agreed. "I'd be glad to go with you."

Saturday came and Jenny picked up Bobby. They listened to some music on the radio and talked some. They'd discussed different things during the summer when they'd played cards with Angus and Timothy. They had learned a number of things about each other at that time.

On the drive, they further discussed things about their families. Jenny spoke of her uncle, her mother and her dad. She told Bobby that her mother and father grew up in Weidman. They got married when they were few months out high school at the United Methodist Church in Weidman. She was born a year after they were married, in November of 1959. Jenny's dad was ten years younger than her uncle Calvin Wilson. Uncle Calvin and her aunt Eva had three children: Calvin Junior who was 31 years old, Roy the middle son at 28 and Ethan, who was the youngest son and 26 at this time. All drove truck for Calvin or worked with his land development machinery. Uncle Calvin developed two subdivisions with his lifelong friend Howard Monroe. After Jenny's parents were married, her dad work for Jenny's uncle for two years driving a truck. Then her dad and her uncle had a falling out. No one including Jenny's mom ever told her what it was about. Jenny's dad obtained a job in Big Rapids working for the Hush Puppy Factory in town. A friend of her dad's was a foreman at the plant and used his influence to get Carl the job. They purchased a small house in Big Rapids.

In May of 1964, he decided to join the army. He was stationed at Fort Benning, Georgia until August of 1965. Jenny said she remembered some things about living in Georgia and starting school there. Carl was sent to Vietnam in August of 1965. Jenny said she remembered leaving her dad, and her mom crying when they left him and crying on the way home on the flight home to Big Rapids. Her dad was killed by enemy fire in October of 1966. She said she remembered all her relatives crying at the funeral, including her Uncle Calvin, but her mother remained stoic during the time before the funeral, at the funeral and after the funeral.

She said, "To this day, my mom will not speak of anything to do with my dad."

Her Aunt Eva said she thought it might be because she didn't want Carl to go into the army to begin with.

After her dad's death, she and her mother had moved in with her Uncle Calvin and Aunt Eva. Her mother began working for her brother Calvin driving a truck and performing other tasks when needed. Her mother rented their house out to college students. She attended Chippewa Hills School through seventh grade. Then they moved back to Big Rapids when Jenny's mom married Angus MacGee's dad. Angus's dad was at instructor at Ferris in the Technical and Arts program.

Angus's mother and his mother's brother were killed in a plane crash. The plane was owned by her mother's brother. They crashed on the way to go hunting for deer in the upper peninsula of Michigan.

After Jenny's mother Martha married Amos MacGee, she enter the nursing program, and when she completed the program, she took a job at Big Rapids Hospital.

Bobby already knew some of the things about which she spoke to him, but Jenny filled in the blanks with more information. They also discussed Bobby's background. When they arrived at Calvin's business, Jenny's uncle came out to greet them. Bobby's eyes popped. Calvin Wilson was a 6'7" 300-pound muscular man. Carl and Bobby hit it off well. They talked for some time while Jenny went into the office and talked to her Aunt Eva.

Calvin, Bobby, Eva and Jenny walked through the truck and land development equipment storage area to the Wilson's home and enjoyed a great lunch.

After lunch, Calvin asked Bobby, "How old are you?"

Bobby answered, "I'm 20. I'll be 21 in September."

Calvin said, "Since Jenny is driving, how about a beer?"

"I've never even tasted beer," Bobby replied. "My dad drinks one sometimes."

"That's great, son," said Calvin with a grin. "I've tasted a few beers over the years."

A dog came walking in. Bobby asked, "Who is he?"

Calvin said, "That's old Fred. He understands English but doesn't speak English."

Bobby and Jenny talked some more on the way home. Bobby said, "Your Aunt Eva sure can cook."

"I told you we would be eating at a great place in Weidman," Jenny replied.

Bobby said, "Your uncle is a really a smart man. I don't remember ever meeting someone who is so well read and knowledgeable in a variety of subjects. He never shows off, either."

Jenny's smiled. "Not bad for I guy who quit school in eleventh grade."

Bobby said, "He also told me, the family unit is very important to him."

When they returned, Jenny left Bobby off at his apartment. Bobby said, "Well, that was a fun day. I'm glad you asked me to go along with you."

Jenny said, "My pleasure. It was nice to see you again. See you around."

"You, too, Jenny," said Bobby.

*

Valentine's day, 1981.

Bobby went home to Anytime. Jaden Rose had set him up with the sister of one of his teammates on the basketball team over Christmas vacation in 1980. Her name was Cheryl Madison and she was from Bloomington, Indiana. Her dad had been a firefighter. He's lost his life at a hotel fire in Bloomington when Cheryl was four years old, and her brother Ernie was six years old. Cheryl was a sophomore at Western Michigan University. When Cheryl was eight years old, her mother married Al Collins, a man who owned a car dealership in Bloomington. He was five years younger than Cheryl's mother. When Cheryl was ten years old, her stepbrother Wally was born. Jaden felt Bobby and Cheryl had some things in common, so he introduced them.

He had kept in touch with her since Christmas. Mollie and Timothy spent time together during most of their free time, so they didn't know about Cheryl. Bobby was home for his dad's birthday, which was the 12th of February. He also had his interview for a job at the Borgess Hospital therapy group. Bobby thought Cheryl was a nice lady, so he decided to spend time with her on Valentine day. Bobby bought her a plant because Cheryl like to grow things.

While spending the day together and going out to dinner, Cheryl opened up about her life. Cheryl told Bobby on this occasion that her life didn't appear to be as great as his.

She said her stepdad wasn't the best guy in the world and she and her brother didn't have the best relationship with him. She said, "It sounds like Mr. Sanborn is a great dad. You call him your dad and he calls you, his son. The day before Mr. Collins married my mom, he told my brother and me never to call him dad, only Al or Mr. Collins. Wally gets away with murder. He has always provided for us but has never been involved in our lives. He never came to our school events or graduations. He allowed our mother to go, but he wouldn't go with her."

She and her brother had scholarships for their education so they never had to asked him for money for college, and yet he was very involved with his son Wally.

Bobby said, "That's sad. I don't remember my biological father, but Dave is my dad and Carrie is my sister. Carrie is a stinker sometimes, but she is a great sister."

"My biological father is known as a hero around Bloomington," Cheryl said with a sigh. "But Al doesn't like it when anyone talks about him."

Bobby and Cheryl had great time together.

Jaden and Sherlee could see how Bobby came out of his shell around Cheryl and talked freely with her. Cheryl and Bobby kept in touch throughout the remaining portion February and the month of March.

*

Easter, 1981.

Bobby and his family went to church at the Methodist Church in Anytown. Angie and Dick Vogel and Buck and Jane Rose were also present. The Vogel's cousin Aubrey Vogel was with them. Aubrey grew up in Madison, Wisconsin but was born in Michigan. Her folks left Anytown when she was three years old. Her father Albert, who was Dick and Angie Vogel's uncle, took a job at a large dairy farm as general manager there.

When she was ten years of age, Aubrey saw Bobby with his family in church at Christmastime. She was with her family, as they were spending Christmas with the Vogel's. Her dad kept in touch with Jane Vogel by visiting her on an occasional weekend to make sure the family was doing okay. Aubrey had six siblings. Her parents did what they could to help Jane, Dick and Angie, but they didn't have a bunch of money to spare, either. Aubrey would come along on these visits with her dad, and she saw Bobby a few times during these visits. Aubrey was very a beautiful 5'9" young lady with long brunette hair. Aubrey and Bobby would have short conversations over the years, typical conversations between Bobby and the opposite sex.

Aubrey always liked the Anytown area, so after she graduated, she obtained a job in 1978 at the tree nursery owned by the Ponci's. John Richmond heard they had a position for a salesperson. Buck Rose had mentioned to him that Aubrey was looking for a job in the area. Aubrey had told Jane that she was attracted to Bobby, so after church, Aubrey invited Bobby to join her in watching her three younger siblings, his sister Carrie and her cousin Angie color Easter eggs.

Bobby said, "I guess I could. It'll give me something to do this afternoon."

Bobby and Aubrey watched for a bit then they decided to go outside and sit on a bench under an oak tree in the back yard. They talked for an extended amount of time. Bobby didn't have any classes on Monday, so he had breakfast with Aubrey, and they talked some more about their careers and life in general. The afternoon found Bobby driving to Big Rapids back to school.

Bobby received letters from both Aubrey and Cheryl through April and May. He returned some of their letters and telephoned each of them a couple of times. His final season of baseball and college studies kept him from too much socializing.

The June 2nd graduation was held at Top Taggart football field. George, Thomas, Timothy, Mollie, Dale and Jaden were in attendance. Bobby's family was there. Cheryl and Aubrey were also there. Jenny and Angus also graduated.

Cheryl and Aubrey both being there made for an interesting development after the ceremony. They each came up and hugged him. Bobby thanked them for coming and simply introduced them to each other and left to join his family. Theresa Williams was also there but stayed in the background and left after noticing him with his group of friends and family. After having a meal with his friends and family, Bobby returned to his apartment, sat down in a chair and laid his head back, relaxing a moment until Mollie and Timbo came in.

Mollie started giggling. She said, "My goodness, Robert, you dog. That sure was different, two ladies coming to your graduation and you acting as if it was no big deal. I wouldn't be happy if I were either one of them."

Bobby shrugged. " it was awfully nice of them to come, but I didn't make a commitment to either of them. I never told either one of them that I had any feelings for them beyond friendship."

Bobby then said, "If you guys you will excuse me, I have something to do. I'll be back."

Mollie said to Timothy, "Well, he avoided that."

Timbo just laughed.

Mollie glared at him. "I don't think it's funny."

Bobby knocked on Jenny's door and her mom answered.

"Come on in," Cindy said. "Jenny is playing euchre with Angus, her dad and Angus's girlfriend in the kitchen."

Bobby hurried into the kitchen.

Jenny asked, "What brings you here, Mr. Stone?"

"I need to talk to you."

Jenny said, "well talk away," Jenny said with a grin.

Bobby winced and said, "I need to talk to you alone."

Jenny looked at the others with wide eyes and said, "This sounds serious."

Bobby asked, "You want get a Coke or something?"

Jenny said, "Sure. Sounds good. I always enjoy your company."

Bobby didn't say much to Jenny on the way to the restaurant. Jenny thought the man who had once been in his shell had gone back into it and she must have made him mad at her. He hadn't said much to her over the last few months and now he was going to tell her why.

They reached the College Food and Drink Court. Bobby pulled out the chair for her to sit down, and then he sat down. He said, "I guess I'll get right to it. I've never told a girl this before. I love everything about you. You are everything I've ever wanted in a woman. Will you marry me?"

"Why, you sly old fox," Jenny exclaimed. "You've got a different girl in every corner and you want to marry me."

Bobby said, "You were the only one ever in my corner."

"I fell in love with you hours after I met you, Bobby," Jenny admitted. "You're one great guy. Of course I will marry you."

When he returned to the apartment, Mollie and Timothy were watching television. Mollie was still upset over what she felt was two-timing, which only made Timbo laugh again.

Mollie glared at Timbo. "I told you it's not funny."

Timbo said, "Well, technically he was three-timing. He just asked Jenny to marry him. I hope she said yes."

Mollie gaped, her eyes sparkling in delight. "You're kidding me."

Timbo grinned and said, " Bobby told me this morning what was going to do."

Bobby said, "I told you, Mollie. I never intentionally led on either Aubrey or Cheryl. I spent some time with them, and I had some nice conversation with them. However, I spoke of Jenny several times during these conversations. I kept in contact with them just like I would any of my buds, but they always initiated any contact we had. Although I admit I did ask Cheryl out on Valentine day."

"Okay, Robert," Mollie said. "But for someone who was rather shy around the ladies, you sure had women surrounding you."

Robert reported to work at Borgess Hospital in July of 1981. Jenny obtained a job working for a trucking company located in Nearbytown in August of 1981.

Robert and Jenny were married in July of 1982 at the Methodist Church in Weidman, Michigan. Timothy was Robert's best man and Angus was the groomsman. Jenny's best friend Alice Jamison was the maid of honor and Andre Wilson, Ethan Wilson's wife, was the bridesmaid.

Bobby and Jenny had two children: a girl named Janet born in 1984 and a boy named Carl born in 1986.

In 1988, Jenny obtained a job teaching high school students mechanical trades at the Vocational Education Center in the county where Anytown was located.

A couple of Major League baseball scouts took a look at Bobby during his college career, but nothing ever came of it.

*

JADEN ROSE graduated from Western Michigan University in June of 1981 with a B.S. degree in economics. He obtained his Master's degree in economics in January of 1983. Sherlee Brown also graduated from Western in June of 1981 with a degree in education. She obtained a job thereafter as a history teacher at Sometown District High School. Sherlee and Jaden were married in August of 1981. After Jaden received his Master's Degree, Sherlee obtained her Master's in Administration in 1985.

Buck Rose purchased a building in Sometown in 1979 and put a furniture business in the lower level of the building. Flooring materials were available in the upper level of the building. Jane (Vogel) Rose managed the furniture and flooring store. Appleton Jenkins (Jade's husband) and Bo Washington installed flooring materials in homes. Jade performed the bookkeeping for both establishments and worked with her dad, Buck, in the entertainment store, where they sold televisions, musical equipment and like items. The installation of antennas had decreased due to the beginning of cable installations. Television repair had also slowly decreased over the years.

Sherlee would sometimes work weekends when needed at both locations during the school year. She worked summers after she obtain her master's degree.

Kyle Schmidt also worked as a salesman at both locations.

Sherlee became Elementary School Principal at the Sometown District in 1990 and High School Principle in the Sometown District in 1996.

Sherlee and Jaden built their home in a remote area. The home overlooked Lake Michigan. Trees covered a great deal of the area. They built their home a substantial distance from the drop-off to Lake Michigan to protect erosion. This had been suggested by Mollie Clausen, the representative of the Environmental Division of the Heath Department. There was extensive drive from the road to the area where their home area existed. The house was beautiful. There was a large gazebo where they could entertain their friends.

Jaden, Sherlee, Willie and Diana Rose moved into the home in July of 1989. When Sherlee and Jaden were home with their children the world took on a positive feeling. The pressures of life became manageable when spending some time there. Jaden and Sherlee said they wanted to have a place where they could breathe the fresh air and relax. There were six bedrooms in the house with six bathrooms, one connected to each bedroom.

Jaden said, "We're paying rent to the bank for our home."

Willie said more than once when he was a small fry, when people would stay overnight at their house, "You won't need to wait to go potty in our house."

Diana would say, "Oh, Willie, you are so gross. That's your son, Dad."

Jaden also said more than once, "Diana, you're just like your mother. Every time you children do something she thinks is inappropriate or troublesome, she says you guys are my children, but when you do something good, you two are her children."

Buck, Jane and Angie lived in the house that Buck, Jade and Jaden lived in when they moved from Chicago. The home was 80 years old, but Buck had made some improvements over time.

John Richmond obtained his builder's license and started building houses 1981. Pat Simmons and Arnie Stokes, who was John's and Buck's senior point guard on their 1979/80 team, worked for John building houses and doing carpentry work. Gary Maeder obtained his Master Electrician's license and Ed Newton obtained his Master Plumber's license. They both worked with John when he needed them to perform their requested professional work.

John Richmond said he'd help Buck build him a new house at a reasonable price. Buck said he and Jane were satisfied with their existing home. Jane rented out the residence she, Angie and Richard had lived in prior to her marrying Buck. Then Richard live in it when he married Marsha Ward, Miller Ward's sister who taught first grade at Sometown School District.

Miller and Richard took trips on motorcycles for a week and a half to various location beginning in the summer of 1989.

*

Bo Washington and Gabby Richmond had a number of successful seasons coaching women's basketball. In 1993, Bo left coaching at Anytown to take a job coaching men's basketball at Camden High School. He also opened a flooring business at a location between Kalamazoo and Battle Creek, Michigan. Jaden Rose was hired to replace Bo. Gabby was still the assistant because her duties as principal didn't allow her to perform any more coaching duties than being the assistant coach for women's basketball.

The 1999 season began with the Anytown women's basketball team losing the first three out of four games. They lost the first game by ten points and the second game by eleven points. The third they won by two points. The fourth they lost by six points. A 5'9" young sophomore by the name of Kathleen Riley and another 6'2" sophomore by the name of Diana Rose were brought up to varsity for the 1999 season. Kathleen averaged 16 points per game on junior varsity. She was as talented at handling the ball as her dad had been and was a very good three-point shooter. Diana Rose averaged 20 points per game on junior varsity.

The fifth game just before Christmas break was with Sometown. Sherlee had mixed emotions about Diana playing basketball for Anytown. She was, of course, employed and had graduated from Sometown, so her allegiance was to the Comets. Diana and Willie went to Sometown, Diana through eighth grade and Willie through seventh grade. Sherlee would drop Willie and Diana off at the Anytown District prior to going to work in the Sometown District. Sherlee and Jaden had a lengthy discussion about this arrangement prior to the making the change. Jaden won out because he wanted to coach his children. Sometown had a respectable women's basketball team, but Sherlee felt they would have been a better than average team with Diana on the team. Ben Spencer and Miller Ward, both players from the 1976-77 Sometown Men's basketball team, coached the Sometown Comets.

Another young lady, a freshman named Janet Stone, was brought up to varsity for the Sometown game. Janet and Kathleen were good at defense and handling the ball. They could shoot from the point area with a great deal of consistency.

Robert Stone also had mixed emotions regarding losing three of his starters off his junior varsity team. The Lady Hawks won the game with the Lady Comets. Jaden worked the three ladies into games as relief for the juniors and seniors on the team. Slowly, as the season went on, Jaden started each game with the senior and junior players. After the thirteenth game, all three players started the games together. The Kiddy Kore, as the rest of the team called them, helped the team win 12 games and lose one game. They won their district championship but lost in the last game of the regional competition. In the 2000 season, they lost in the quarterfinals to Bay City All Saints. Mollie Clausen also had her moments of mixed feelings but sat with the Hawks fans.

Mollie and Timothy went to the semifinal game, Bay City lost to Detour from the Upper Peninsula of Michigan. Kathleen, Diana and Janet won the State Championship in 2001. All the members of the 1977 Championship team were at the game.

Tammy Clausen played some basketball her senior year (2001). This was the only year she played. She substituted when needed at a variety of positions down low. Tammy was good at rebounds but she didn't have the best shot outside. Her points were from gathering rebounds. The Kiddy Kore and her parents talked her into playing her senior year. She didn't play in every game because cross country conflicted a few times. Tim Clausen was the cross country and track coach, appointed in 1994.

Tammy and her dad ran in some marathons together during the summer months. Tammy's sport was track and cross country. She won several honors in both of these sports. She won the mile run at the State meet three years in row.

Lee Patrick Clausen was the starting quarterback his sophomore year for the 2001 football team at Anytown.

Ed Clausen retired from coaching and teaching in 1996 but still did some scouting for both men's and women's basketball teams with Kyle Schmidt.

*

Kyle Schmidt obtained his barber's license in 1988 and was now the barber in town. He worked with Everette Perkins until Mr. Perkins retired in 1991 at the age of 81. Everette developed a muscle weakening disease in 1989 and passed away in 2000. He attended basketball games until a short time before he passed and gave away combs to all his customers for four months prior to his last day at the barbershop. He said the combs were "parting gifts."

Kyle had developed a customer following from Sometown as result of his time spent working for Buck at the furniture store and entertainment store. The barbershop and *Jack's Place* continued be the gathering places for The Crew over the years, with new members from the Alum. They expressed their thoughts each year regarding the athletic teams. At times, the customers from Sometown would cross paths at the shop to discuss athletic subjects, including who had better team. Some betting also occurred among customers from both towns during these visits.

*

JOHN RICHMOND and BUCK ROSE still coached men's basketball for Anytown in 2002. They never won another State Championship, but they never had a losing season. Their team won the regionals in 1993 and 1994 when John's sons Ben and Jimmy played on the team. Anytown won their district 24 times from 1975 to 2001. Those years they didn't win the district, they still had a winning record. They recorded several wins in the regionals over the years, even when not advancing to the regional final or winning the regional final game. Buck and John always made sure those players who made the team played an appropriate amount of time if they could get them in. They made sure all the players felt like part of the team. Several years, a number of players became overachievers based on their talent and athletic abilities.

John's sons also played football for Buck Rose and had successful years.

John and Gabby built a house on the other side of Clear Lake across from Jim Klein's property.

Tony Ponzi's son Ed and Pat Simmons took over operating the vending machines business. The business became very successful, covering four counties with a large number of accounts in every county.

John and Gabby, Charles and Irene played golf together for several years. Thomas and June Decker would occasionally play with both couples. Thomas won the Club Champion in 1994, 1995, 1996 and 1987. Buck, John, Charles and Thomas played in number of four-person scrambles. June, Gabby, Irene and Mollie also played in these four-person scrambles. A few times, Irene and Gabby played with Thomas and Buck in these scrambles. John began having troubles with his leg in later years and his scores weren't as good. Charles also had some problems of his own with his arm as time went on.

*

MOLLIE CLAUSEN became the Director of the Environmental Health Division of the county health department in 1999, one the first female directors. Mollie had a number of experiences along the way, working in a county where her husband grew up and friends and family of her husband would cross paths with her.

One experience was with Morrie Jenkins and his son Perry. Mollie had an encounter regarding the raising of pigs. Several homes had been built on Jenkins Lake over the years. Since the turn of the 20th century, the Jenkins family owned most of the property around the lake, hence the name Jenkins Lake.

The Jenkins family subdivided much of the property during the 1960's. In the 1980's, several homes were built around the lake. The Jenkins had sawmill on the property which they maintained. In 1976, Morrie decided to close the sawmill and decided go into the business of raising pigs on a small scale. At first, it was interesting for the families who owned homes on the lake to watch the piglets being born. Perry Jenkins also sold the pork to the families for a reasonable price.

Then, in the late 1980's, houses on the lake tripled. In 1985, it was discovered that on hot days the pigs were occasionally allowed to bathe the in the lake. The population of the pigs had also tripled. In 1984, a Lake Association was formed. They made a complaint to Mollie regarding the bathing situation in July of 1985. After the first complaint, a fence was installed. In September, the pigs broke through the fence. This problem was solved by Perry building a board fence around the direct area of the lake.

Several complaints continued for one thing or another. Then in July, Perry obtained some candy bars from a company in Battle Creek who need to dispose of a number of batches because they didn't meet standards. This product was stored in a portion of the sawmill structure. Bees gathered in swarms in the area along with other insects. This again summoned Mollie to the property. The following day, the candy was taken to a landfill. Soon afterward, the entire pig population was sold to Mollie's relief.

*

BOBBY RILEY played basketball all four years of his high school attendance. He played point guard and secondary guard. He was seventh or six man depending on the situation. He was an excellent ball handler, just like his dad George. Basketball was the only sport in which Bobby participated. Hunting and fishing were more enjoyable for him and his brother Billy.

Billy won a trout fishing contest when he was 16 and a bass fishing contest when he was 17. Billy was an outstanding fly-fisherman. Billy also played baseball and was an excellent first baseman. He had a 486 batting average with 22 home runs in his high school career.

Jim Klein semi-retired in 1993 from fruit farming. At this point, George took over the day-to-day operations of the business fulltime. Billy and Bobby worked for their dad during their teens. When Billy graduated from high school, he worked with his dad fulltime. Bobby worked with his grandfather Daniel in the insurance business when he graduated from high school. Jill, George's sister, took over managing the paperwork of the fruit growing business after she graduated from Western Michigan University in 1984.

Jill married Terry Cowens in 1985. Terry drove a race car at the local raceway. Charles Decker and Daniel Riley sponsored him in his endeavors. Terry won races several times over the years.

June Decker, Billy and Daniel sold insurance out of the offices in Anytown and Niles, Michigan. Both offices and the office for the fruit farm were adorned with trophies from fishing and hunting. Each trophy had a review of who, how and when each fish had been caught or each animal was shot. Billy's awards for fishing contests were also on display.

Terry was also presented with several awards for his racing triumphs, and these were also displayed. These trophies and awards provided conversation with the clients who visited the office.

*

WILLIE ROSE's class was asked by their eighth-grade English teacher to write an essay on a subject of their choice. Being a boy, Willie chose to write about high school sports. Willie would hang with his dad Jaden at girls' basketball practices or football practices with his grandpa Buck in the fall after school when he didn't have practice himself with junior high football. In the winter, you'd find him at the boys' basketball practices with John Richmond and Buck or at volleyball practices when he didn't have junior high basketball practice.

He therefore wrote an essay on high school sports. He wrote:

High school football, basketball, volleyball, baseball and softball may be played at public schools or parochial schools whether rich or poor. Each participant will recall a special time, a moment when his or her specific play was particularly successful. This play will forever remain special for them. These plays will be discussed again and again. A visit to the local barbershop and other locations may provide an ear for listening to the discussion of one's favorite moments. The discussion may revolve around an upside occurrence or a downside occurrence. Sometimes these stories or discussions may be indulged. As the years go on, sometimes these moments may be embellished. My grandpa and dad have admitted that they and others may have been guilty of these embellishments throughout the years.

The essence is something which cannot be duplicated. Current players or alumni of a school can provide the history of a game or event. These memories are therefore preserved.

Willie decided after completing eighth grade at Anytown to return to complete his high school education at Sometown. He enjoyed his time at Anytown, and he had many friends, but he wanted to play sports representing Sometown with friends he'd made as he grew up with them in elementary school.

As we already know, Diana chose to stay at Anytown to play for her dad. Willie had considered playing for his grandpa on the football team, but his friends won out. He had kept in touch with many of them during his time attending Anytown.

Willie became an outstanding quarterback. He was a 6'3", two-hundred-pound muscular individual in his sophomore year. He had an excellent freshman year in all sports. He really started to excel beginning in his sophomore year. Willie set records at Sometown in passing yardage, touchdown passes and running for a quarterback. He scored several points running for touchdowns and extra points.

Lee Mogg, the son of Earl Mogg, and Devin Moore, the son of Gene Moore, and the M & M Twins from the 1974/75 basketball team were players who caught 95% of Willie's passes throughout their high school careers.

Willie was also a better-than-average basketball player and track member, but football was his sport. Buck lost all three games Willie played against Buck's team, though the final scores were always close. In Willie's senior year against Anytown, the final score was 42-38. The game was spectacular, with Willie passing for four touchdowns, running for two touchdowns and running for three extra points.

Patrick Lee Clausen also had an excellent game passing. He threw four touchdowns. Freshman Carl Stone ran for a 50-yard touchdown.

Buck rushed over to the Sometown sidelines after the game and hugged Willie. Every year regarding each football game between Sometown and Anytown that Willie played in, Buck and Willie had a bet—the loser had to rake the winner's yard. Willie was awarded All-State first team his junior and senior years in football, awarded second team All-State in basketball his senior year and was state champion in the 100-yard dash at the state track meet his junior and senior years.

*

In 1998, MAUREEN and DALE RICHTER were as happy a married couple could be.

Dale said to his dad Scott, "Everything about Maureen has made everything about me better."

They shared their joy with others at a gathering on their 15th wedding anniversary. Maureen gave Dale an album of their most precious moments with their children for Dale's office. Dale baked heart-shaped cookies for the event. After the event and the children were tucked in their beds, Dale covered the small table in front of the fireplace with rose petals and they both drank wine from goblets.

Dale spent all his free time away from court proceedings with Maureen and his children. They spent their summer weekends at their summer getaway place at Lake Huron. Dale grilled items for the family and then they'd eat their meals on a picnic table Scott and Dale had made. Maureen would purchase watermelons and the family would have watermelon seed spitting contests. Dale would play his guitar, and they'd sing everyone's favorite songs. When he came home from work, Dale would play his guitar by himself for half an hour in the den of their house and then would have his children come in and sing with him. Maureen would sometimes also join them. Dale would then question each child about their school day and their homework.

Several times, Patricia Richter told her brothers Carl and Scott that they smelled. Her sister Camille would also chime in sometimes and agree with her big sister. Patricia wasn't Peppermint Patty, but she was more like Lucy van Pelt of Peanuts fame as she could be bossy at times. She ruled the roost.

Camille looked up to her big sister—Carl and Scott, not so much. But being 5'8" tall and Carl and Scott being much smaller, they allowed her to dominate them. Patricia was much like her mother Maureen regarding saying what was on her mind. Carl, Scott and Camille enjoyed playing and just being together with Patricia.

Dale and Maureen challenged their children to do their best in everything they did, but taught them to be good sports when winning along with accepting defeat. Good grades were important, but the effort was more important the final outcome.

One night after they ate, Dale brought them all together to discuss the "smell" comments. He felt enough was enough

Dale explained, "Boys and girls, scientists tell us that air is filled with odor molecules. They enter your nasal cavity every time you breathe. Just behind the nose, these molecules are absorbed by mucous-covered tissue. This tissue is covered with receptor cells which stick out and wave in the air currents we inhale. Forty of them must detect odor molecules before a smell is registered. When a new smell is detected, the tiny olfactory bulb located just above the cavity flashes data directly into the limbic system, which handles feelings, instincts and invention. The limbic system may provoke powerful emotions, images or nostalgia. It has been said that girls and women have a keener sense of smell than boys and men. It has also been said that by simply smelling a piece of clothing, most people can tell if it was worn by a woman or a man."

Scott injected, "That may be because women wear makeup and perfume more often than men."

That brought a smile to everyone's face.

Patricia said, "Okay, Dad. I won't teel the boys they smell anymore."

The children all knew this was Dale's method of telling them to stop doing something inappropriate.

These initial explanations Dale gave at these sessions were intended to be educational, but they were for the most part meant to explain that they'd better not continue the offense in the future. Sometimes the children didn't understand all the terminology but they knew any future transgressions regarding the particular offense would mean more point penalties.

These sessions were sometimes given as group and other times individually.

The Richter children were considered excellent students in school. Patricia showed signs of being a good athlete. She performed well when participating in athletic events. Scott and Carl showed signs of being better-than-average athletes, particularly in baseball. They both were short in stature but could have grown with time as both their parents had. Camille was tall for her age and showed signs of talent with the basketball. The track coaches at the children's school had their eyes on her because of the speed she showed in a physical skills tests and the annual spring track events held for elementary school students.

*

THOMAS and JUNE DECKER'S children weren't born with the concerns Irene and Charles had with Thomas at birth. Precautions had been taken when June became pregnant to rule out any problems.

The twins Jacob and Josephine were not only different being female and male but in other ways, as well. Josephine was a tomboy like her grandmother. Jacob enjoyed the arts and nature. Josephine learned to play golf at eight years old. Jacob took dance lessons at the same age. Jacob wasn't interested golf but did like to ride along in the cart to witness nature within the surroundings. Jacob enjoyed playing soccer and was a better-than-average athlete at the sport. Jacob love to grow things and helped June with her garden. Josephine disliked hoeing and weeding.

Josephine played softball in the summer program in Anytown. Jacob spent time at the library and playing chess with his friend Alexander Andrews either at his house or Alexander's house. Jacob acted in plays at the local playhouse in Nearbytown, while Josephine and Jacob liked to go to the races with their parents to watch their Uncle Terry Cowens, but Jacob would take a book about history to read. Josephine played football, baseball and basketball with the boys at recess. Jacob did play baseball and kickball. He enjoyed playing marbles when he was in third and fourth grade.

Jacob played trumpet in the band. Josephine and Jacob both sang in the church choir. Josephine had good grades, and Jacob had excellent grades. Josephine joked that her favorite subject in school was recess. Jacob had good citizenship and was a class leader while Josephine was sometimes a leader in mischief. Jacob loved watching history and westerns on television. Josephine and Jacob would watch westerns together.

Josephine liked to watch sporting events. She enjoyed eating tomatoes and corn, but Jacob didn't like tomatoes and corn. Jacob like peas and cucumbers. Josephine didn't like peas and cucumbers. They both liked to play board games together, especially Trivial Pursuit. Josephine would challenge anyone who would pick on Jacob.

Jacob and Josephine like to play with Kathleen and Daniel. When Jacob was asked by Clare Kinney to kiss her when they were nine years old, he kissed her on the forehead. He told Clare it was a cultured kiss and was all she'd get from him.

Thomas felt that Jacob might be a Dale Richter in athletics. He needed to be slowly guided into sports. Thomas said he believed Jacob showed signs of developing into a good basketball player.

One time when they met for lunch, Thom told George and Timbo that he'd spent some time with both Jacob and Josephine running them through drills. He said he felt their performance was a good ruler for measuring their abilities.

Timbo quipped, "A tape measure is a good measurement for their height, also."

George said, "Timbo, you're always available for comment, aren't you?"

Thom added that he knew Josephine liked sports, but when he'd once asked Jacob if he liked sports, he'd answered, "I like hamburgers and French fries more. Participating in sports is good way to work off the calories you put in your body. However, bowling and shooting pool put in more calories because of the food and refreshment you consume during those activities. Even so, bowling is entertainment for your *spare* time." Jacob further said, "If I have to try sports I will, but it will be *trying*."

George said, "Timbo, it looks as if Jacob may give you a run for your money with smart-aleck remarks."

Thom said, "Josephine, is just as quick with the quips. One day when we were eating dinner, I asked her how school was that day and she said, 'Well, Mr. Langely was talking about something in history and went on and on about the same thing. It was as if there was a loud noise and then nothing, or then nothing and the loud noise stopped.'"

*

BOBBY STONE organized his children and those of Dale, Thomas, Jaden, George and Timothy for the purpose of playing a flag football game and a four-on-four basketball game. The football game was played on a field located on his ten acres of property on Saturday afternoon, and the basketball game was played at Scott La Roque's basketball court on Sunday of Memorial day weekend, 2002.

Scott had stopped raising beef cattle in 1990. He'd converted his barn into a basketball facility with basketball hoops and backboards at each end of the upper portion of the barn. Over the years, the La Roque court was a hangout for several boys and girls in the area to play the game.

Bobby and Jaden developed the teams. They were as follows:

Jaden's team: Katheen Riley, Janet Stone, Josephine Decker, Bobby Riley, Willie Rose, Carl Richter and Jacob Decker.

Bobby's team: Tammy Clausen, Diana Rose, Patricia Richter, Billy Riley, Carl Stone, Scott Richter and Lee Patrick Clausen.

Willie Rose was the quarterback of his team and Lee Patrick Clausen played the same position for the other team. Jacob Decker was the center for his team. Patricia Richter played the same position for her team. Bobby and Jaden would switch the players around based on what plays Willie or Lee Patrick called.

They played for two-and-a-half hours. They kept score for some time and then they just played. Tammy Clausen's speed was an advantage for passing plays for her team. Bobby Riley's ability to get open for a pass was an advantage to his team.

The basketball games were somewhat more competitive than the football game. Some liberties were taken when Carl Richter, Patricia Richter, Jacob Decker, Josephine Decker and Scott Richter had the ball when they dribbled and shot. The defense was casual when they had the ball. When the other players had possession of the basketball, the defense was very tight. The four-on-four games were played for four hours. Nine games were played with the first team to ten points the winner.

Bobby's team won five games and Jaden's team won four.

*

There was a manmade lake created in 1981 located between Sometown and Anytown. There was a raised portion of land in the middle of the lake which formed an island. This was where the County Fair was now held. There was a Pavilion where gatherings were held. A portable stage was provided for entertainment in front of an outdoor auditorium.

When the stage wasn't present, baseball games were held for the local high school games and other baseball games. Dugouts for each team were present flanking the auditorium. A fence surrounded the entertainment/baseball complex.

The property was named *Island Park and Fairgrounds*.

A picnic was held here for the families of the team members. Carrie Sanborn Joravsky was present with her husband Niles Joravsky. She was on leave from the Navy. She had reached the rank of Lieutenant

Commander. She and Niles didn't have any children. Niles worked as a marketing representative for Hormel Foods in Virginian Beach, Virginia.

Angie Vogel married Arthur Johnson, Harold Johnson's grandson from *J and J's Grocery*, now *J and J's Food Market and Pharmacy*. Arthur and his brother Harold were the pharmacists and owned half of the business with Scott La Roque. Angie and Arthur had one son, age three, named Norman. Angie managed the financial portion of the pharmacy.

Aubrey Vogel Ponzi was also in attendance. Every year, Bobby Stone, Timbo Clausen, Thomas Decker and Jaden Rose went up to Tony's cabin near Hancock, Michigan to hunt deer. Dale didn't hunt deer and George never could get away because had to take care of the cold storage of fruit operations.

Everyone went swimming and enjoyed beef burgers, hot dogs, fried fish, venison burgers, grilled turkey, potato salad and Mary Klein Riley's cherry pies and apple pies.

*

GAIL JENKINS died in 1990.

Gail Jenkins and Frank Baker had hired Amelia Martin Ward to clean house and performed other duties around the house starting in 1984. Gail still cooked and baked until 1988, when she was diagnosed with breast cancer. At that time, they hired Gail's granddaughter Tina Carson to cook them three meals a day. Toward the end of her life, Frank hired a nurse for Gail.

Everette Perkins asked Frank how he had the means to pay for the various duties.

Frank quipped, "You know that my daughter and son are rich. They have many nuggets."

Frank was also a caregiver within his abilities. At Gail's funeral, Frank spoke about how he was a lucky man to have had a wonderful wife and a wonderful companion over the years. Frank also said, "round 1984, Gail started calling me *honey* and *sugar*. Some people got the idea that we may have been more than companions. I told them we were still living as just companions. One day, I asked her why she'd started calling me those names. Jokingly, she said, 'Because I forgot your name three years ago.'"

In his later years, Frank spent his days first eating breakfast at home and then walking down to the barbershop for some conversation and coffee there. Then he headed over to *Jack's Place* for more conversation until noon. He'd take a short nap and then ate lunch at home. After that he went back to *Jack's* for more conversation, card playing and a couple of beers until around 5 P.M. each day.

One morning back when Gail first started living with Frank, Frank complained that his coffee was cold. Gail said, "It was hot a half hour ago when you asked if the coffee was ready."

After that, Frank was never late when Gail said something along the lines of food or drinks were ready. Even after she became ill, she still made coffee for her and Frank each morning until two months before she passed.

Frank died in 1997 at the age of 101. He followed his daily routine until 1996 when he began to slow down. Irene found him sitting in his recliner with a picture of Emma in his hand the day he passed.

*

On one occasion in 1995, the group decided play some cards in the morning and Frank's card-playing buddies decide to play a little trick on him when he left the table to use the restroom. They gave him a royal flush hand of cards. Frank sat down, looked at his cards and didn't say a word. A couple of his buddies elbowed each other and winked at each other when they didn't have Frank's eye on them. Frank made an opening bet, another bet and then folded.

Because he knew they may in the forefront for the ruse, Frank specifically told Gilbert and Andrew Washington (Bo Washington's granddad) to go home, take a nap and think up something more in depth in trickery.

He said, "I might be way beyond my years of life expectancy, and I may be a physically unsteady character, but my brain still can catch on to a setup."

Gilbert Pauley, who had worked for Frank at his butcher shop, purchased the shop from Frank. Gilbert closed the shop in 1989 and retired. Gilbert's wife died in 1990. He sold his home and move to an apartment in Nearbytown to be near his lifetime friend Frank. He and Frank had visited each other through the years after Frank moved to Anytown. After Gail Jenkins died, Gilbert moved in with Frank.

Irene or Charles would drive Frank to Gilbert's home when he could no longer drive distances farther than around Anytown. Frank called him his excuse buddy, his excuse to leave town.

As stated, Frank was home each day at close to 5 P.M. One day in April, he and Gilbert arrived home at 5:45 P.M. Tina told them they were late.

Frank said, "We're not late. The days are getting longer so you think we're late."

Tina shook her head. "That makes no sense."

Frank said, "At my age, I don't have to make sense."

"Well, sense or no sense, you'd two better arrive home on time or call and say you're going to be late," Tina snapped back.

Frank said, "I understand. We're sorry. It won't happen again."

Frank left a message to be read at his funeral which stated that his family and his friends gave him a grateful life which he'd lived to his fullest. He could now be reunited with beautiful and wonderful Emma. He said he may even enjoy seeing Jacob Decker, Charlie Stone, Abe Sanborn and many others.

Irene spoke at his funeral. She said, "My dad lived in passionate pursuit of knowledge. He was a self-taught man. From a one-room schoolhouse, he put on his hat, gaining wisdom about the nature of life. He projected a gruff exterior, but this masked a loving and caring, devoted family man and a trusted friend. The gruff exterior appeared to be the mannerism of many of my dad's generation, such as my father-in-law Jacob. His family and friends seemed to understand that he had an inner warmth. A one-on-one conversation revealed his joyful and compassionate spirit. When in a group, many times he'd would present a blunt and curt attitude. Although he didn't regularly attend church, he had a deep spiritual faith that guided his life which was garnered by my mother. My dad told my brother and me when we were young that challenges happened in life, and overcoming them is what made life meaningful. He also told us we needed to stand up for what we believed in, because sooner or later the fastest runners had to stand and fight. If we hit rock bottom it sometimes would become a foundation to react and raise our lives up. He reminded us not allow happiness to result in someone's loss."

Irene continued, "Someone asked my dad just recently what his recipe was for his long life. He replied that he lived life just for the love of it. No other answer was needed. Love was like a shelter. If you left life in God's hands, that was all you needed to do. He further said he'd a little hiccup when Emma died, but his family came to his rescue and straightened him out."

"My dad had a good run."

*

ALICE CLAUSEN obtained a teaching position at Anytown, leaving the Perigan school district in 1982.

Alice, Mary Riley and the band director Cecil Barnard Mills instituted a talent venue in April of 1984 which they called *Band Follies*.

Cecil Mills was named after Cecil B. de' Mille. Cecil's grandmother asked that his parents' firstborn if it was a boy, to be named so. Vera Mills loved movies and she often stated that she felt Mr. de'Mille was the greatest filmmaker. She was aware people indicated that he was the father of American filmmaking. He was also considered the most successful producer/director in the film industry. She also believed he was most distinguished filmmaker of epic films.

Vera requested Cecil's parents name their firstborn, if a boy, after Mr. de 'Mille, because she felt if he was introduced to a variety of the arts, he may be successful in the profession. She and her husband Luke had been involved in local productions for a number of years.

Cecil grew up in Reese, Michigan and indeed did become interested in music and drama. He could play several instruments. He met Leslie Brown (Banjo) and Anna Osborne Brown at band-camp. Cecil was involved in the drama department at Central Michigan University and was a member of the band.

After graduation in 1979, he obtained a job at Centerville High School in Michigan as band director. A son of a friend of Josephine Decker was superintendent there. A year after the superintendent retired, an opening for a band director at Anytown occurred in 1983. Cecil had kept Anytown in his mind over years as his favorite place to be besides Reese, Michigan. He kept in touch with Thomas Decker and his family and Banjo and Anna after the camp and had followed the '77 basketball team. He'd attended the championship game. Students could perform such talents as vocals (readings and singing), skits, dances and instrumental performances. The idea was for a student to present any of his or her talents.

During the first year, Carrie Sanborn sang Bonnie Tyler's *Total Eclipse Of The Heart* and did a duet with John Fox, the grandson of Earl Fox, of *Islands in the Stream* by Kenny Rogers and Dolly Parton.

Angie Vogel performed a dance which she'd originally performed at her dance recital in March. The *Who's on First* Abbott and Costello routine was performed a number of times throughout the years. Bobby and Billy Riley performed the routine two years in a row. One year Dianna Rose, Tammy Clausen and Kathleen Riley performed two Supremes songs, *Baby Love* and *Stop in the Name of Love*. Eleven-year-old fifth grader Janet Stone sang *I Will Always Love You* by Whitney Houston. She performed several songs each year thereafter. Tammy Clausen and her friends Sonia Hartman and Barbara Sampsel performed the *Niagara Falls Slowly Turned* skit made famous by the Three Stooges. They also did the little ditty The Three Stooges also performed and the Andrews Sisters did, which went as follows:

Mares eat oats
And does eat oats
And little lambs eat ivy
A kid'll eat ivy, too,
Wouldn't you?

If the words sound queer
and funny to your ear
A little bit of jumble and jivy
Sing: Mares eat oats
And does eat
And little lambs eat ivy.

Another year, she sang *Don't Fence Me In* and *I've Got Spurs that Jingle Jangle.*

Jimmy and Ben Richmond played the piano and sang *I Been Everywhere*, a song originally recorded by Hank Snow and sung by several others. They also performed *Dueling Pianos* with each playing a piano. Gabby had persuaded them each to take lessons. At first, they weren't excited about taking lessons. Then, the more they learned the instrument, the more they enjoyed the experience.

Soon after they took over operating *Jacks Place*, they set up a piano bar with Jimmy and Ben taking requests every Saturday night.

Lee Patrick Clausen put together with his dad Timothy a roast-type skit with Timbo as the one who was roasted.

Regarding Timbo's golf game, Lee said, "When my dad hits the ball right it's a slice. When he hits it left, it's a hook. When he hits it straight, it's miracle."

"The difference between my dad looking for a present for my mom and golf is my dad will look for a golf ball he hit off the fairway for ten minutes."

"My dad hits his woods very well—it's getting out of the woods where he has a problem."

"A man once joined my dad and his friends Mr. Decker and Mr. Rose to make a foursome. My dad hit a few real good shots and the man said he ought to be on tour. Mr. Decker said he would, but he doesn't like to travel."

"My dad carries an auger in his bag so he can get closer to the hole once he gets on the green. My dad is too close to the ball after he hits it. My dad got into poison ivy once—that is as close as he has come to being a scratch golfer. My dad has regripped his ball retriever three times because he has used it so much."

"The doctor told my dad he shouldn't be playing golf. When my mom heard this, she said, 'He must have played with you, Timbo.'"

"Dad always takes two pair of socks with him in case he gets a hole in one. If you want to improve your golf game, take lessons, practice and don't watch what my dad does playing the game."

"My dad and one of his friends were standing on the tee for one hole which overlooked a river to the left of them. They observed two fellows fishing. My dad said, 'Look at those two idiots fishing in the pouring rain.'"

Then Lee told two golf jokes which went like this:

"A man came home from golf tired. His wife asked him why he was so tired. He said, 'Well, my partner Charlie died on the third hole, and after that it was hit the ball and drag Charlie.'"

"A man was playing golf with his buddies when a funeral procession passed by. The man took off his hat and placed it over his heart. One of his friends asked, 'Someone you knew?' The man said, 'We would have been married 45 years in August.'"

Lee finished by quipping, "Golf balls are like eggs. You buy them by the dozen and within two weeks you need to buy another dozen."

*

FRANCES LOUDERMOUTH was born in 1959 in a cotton field near Fayetteville Arkansas. His parents were Leroy and Flossie Laudermouth. Flossie died two days after Frances was born.

Frances was despised and disliked by his father thereafter. Leroy blamed Frances for his wife's death. When Frances was old enough to understand what Leroy was saying, he told Frances on many occasions that he wished Frances had died instead of his mother.

Leroy lived in a beat-up old mobile out in woods 20 miles out of Fayetteville. He had a shallow well for a water source and an outhouse.

Flossie's sister Betty Sue and her husband Colby basically raised Frances, as they were told they couldn't have children. In fact, Betty Sue had a hand in naming Frances. Betty stayed home with Frances while Colby and Leroy worked in the cotton fields.

Betty Sue and Colby Parker lived in a house just a short distance from Leroy's mobile home. When Frances was six years old, Betty Sue and Colby's house caught on fire because Leroy let a small brush fire get out of control after a day of drinking beer and whiskey. The house burned to ground, and Leroy's mobile home was also destroyed. Betty Sue, Colby, Leroy and Frances lived in three of the ten abandoned cars on the property until Leroy found an abandoned boxcar. The boxcar was a remnant in a railroad yard where no-longer-efficient cars were stored. Leroy and Colby negotiated with the railroad to haul the boxcar to their property. They then placed a kitchen, eating room and bedroom in the boxcar. They attached another constructed bedroom and bathroom to the unit.

When Frances was ten years old, Betty Sue and Colby moved to Saginaw, Michigan, where Colby had obtained a job at Saginaw Steering Gear. Leroy relinquished his parental rights to Frances and Colby and Betty Sue adopted him. Colby wasn't the best influence on Frances. He drank heavily when he wasn't working. He did manage to report to work each day, but he was abusive to Betty Sue and Frances whenever he was drinking.

Betty Sue and Flossie had a close friend Leona who had met a man while working in Michigan. They were married and had settled down in Saginaw, Michigan. The man, Gene Higgins, worked at Saginaw Steering Gear and helped Colby get the job at that plant.

Gene and Leona had told Betty Sue to take Frances and leave Colby, but she insisted on staying. Gene told her it wasn't good for Frances to grow up in that environment, nor was it good for Betty Sue.

As time went on, Frances grew more and more rebellious. When he was 13 years old, the Parkers were informed through a friend in Arkansas that Leroy had passed away from a brain hemorrhage two months' prior. Frances showed no emotion but staring for a few minutes. When Frances was 14 years old, Colby died from cancer. Betty Sue did the best she could to control Frances's defiant and lawless attitude, but it was fruitless.

Frances was in and out of trouble with petty crimes. He was caught shoplifting and then breaking and entering and was sent to a juvenile facility for a year when he was 16 years old. After he was released, he still remained defiant.

He managed to earn a high school diploma and then got a job working for a garbage pickup service.

He married Billy Jo Naylor after meeting her on trip down to Arkansas after he lost his job at the garbage service when he 20 years old. His bad attendance record at work had caused him to be fired. He married Billy Jo after knowing her for only two weeks. He brought her back to Saginaw, where she obtained a job as waitress in restaurant just off the interstate. He worked for a farmer who raised sugar beets. They were plagued with financial issues.

One day Frances went in to get a haircut and the barber asked him if he had money to pay for it. He had developed a history of telling people he would pay later if the person would just give him a break. Someone in the shop made a remark about his stiffing people. Frances picked him up and threw him through the barbershop window. In and out of jail became his modus operandi.

Gabe Landers the farmer kept him on because he liked him, and when he reported for work, he did work hard every time.

When he was 21 years old, Frances broke into the restaurant just off the interstate and robbed the establishment. He was sent to jail for two years because of his crime history. After being in jail over a year, he received the news that Billy Jo was pregnant with another man's baby. Along with all his other problems growing up, this pressed him psychologically. A short time after this news, he assaulted another inmate and beat him almost to death, which gave him two more years of jail time. He was still a problem during the next two years. Then with some counseling in his fourth year he became less combative.

When he was released from jail, he had trouble finding a job. He had a series of jobs from 1985 to 1988 and managed to keep out of trouble during this time. Then a day came when could no longer find a job, due again to his work attendance. As a result, he became homeless. A bridge near Saginaw Steering Gear became his home during warm weather and a shelter his home during cold weather. Begging, dumpster salvaging and bottle and can retrieval for deposits became his meager means of survival.

One day in 1989, Betty Sue was driving near the Saginaw Steering Gear factory when she had just left off her husband, Gene Higgins. Leona Higgins had died in 1986 in a car accident. A year later, Gene and Betty Sue were married. Leona and Gene had a daughter and son close to Frances's age. If there was ever a good influence on Frances, Pete and Dorian were.

After his second year in prison, Frances had rejected any contact Betty Sue had attempted to provide and she hadn't seen him since. Betty Sue looked to her left and saw what she thought was Frances. After some cordial initial discussion they went and sat on a nearby bench. After an hour or so, it was agreed Frances would come home with Betty Sue.

Gene had been promoted to plant manager at Saginaw Steering Gear, and Frances stayed with Gene and Betty Sue for a week. Then one day Gene came home and informed Frances that he had two jobs for Frances. Gene said he could either work at his plant or at his brother Arthur Higgins's campground in Cheboygan, Michigan, as Arthur had an opening at his campground as a caretaker. Gene suggested maybe the campground position might be the best because it would be a fresh start. In addition, Arthur would help him get his plumber's license and his electrician's license.

Arthur's wife was a florist and owned a greenhouse. Gene stated that Frances could work during the winter months at the greenhouse. Frances decided to take the caretaker job. Arthur set him up in a unit at the campground for living quarters. After the camping season was over, Frances found an apartment in Cheboygan.

Arthur was a devout Episcopalian. He attended church every Sunday and was a Sunday School Teacher. After a few months Arthur convinced Frances to attend church with him.

In 1990, Frances began dating Anita Cashway from the church, whom he was introduced to after church at a coffee and baked goods gathering. They were married in June of 1991. They had a son named Gavin in September of 1992 and a daughter named Jane in February of 1994.

In 1993, Frances obtained a job with a builder who was a cousin of Arthur's wife Jill, installing plumbing and performing some electrical work.

In 1998, Frances attended a weekend gathering of Catholic and Episcopal men with Arthur. Here he met Dale Richter. After this gathering Frances, Arthur and Dale would meet at least twice a month for breakfast to discuss life's ups and downs with a religious theme.

In October of 2000, Frances and Dale decided walk on a pilgrimage type trip from Mt. Pleasant, Michigan to Saginaw, Michigan. The trip would end at the bridge where Frances had spent his homeless nights. They took the back roads on their journey. It was a wonderful experience. They enjoyed each other's company and enjoyed the sights of nature and the surroundings of the rural areas. The beauty could not be matched.

They discussed all sorts of subjects when camping out at night along the way. Some were religious in matter. The final night was spent overnight under the bridge in Saginaw. Arthur picked them up the following morning and brought them back to Cheboygan.

Dale gave a ten-minute presentation of their journey at the 25th class reunion.

George, Timbo, Bobby, Thom and Jaden had all met Frances at the Girls State Championship game.

Gerry Martin

CHAPTER FOURTEEN

THE REUNION

Classmates came from far and wide to the 25th reunion of the class of 1977 of Anytown School.

The first half hour consisted of handshakes and hugs from the Alumni. A drink of choice either alcoholic or nonalcoholic were provided. There were many exchanges of what had happened in the classmates' lives since the last reunion. A like discussion continued throughout the meal served to the classmates.

As planned, Timbo Clausen was the Master of Ceremonies.

Timbo began the further portion of the festivities by giving the floor to Mary Riley. Mary Riley had provided an *Alumni News* for each classmate which she began publishing and sending to them annually after their fifth class reunion. Mary conducted a trivia game based on the *News* and the class highlights during the days of their time spent in the Anytown school district.

Dale Richter, "Mr. Quiet" during his high school years, and his group around his table, won the competition correctly answering the most questions.

Timbo told group after the trivia game, "A trip to nostalgia is good for the soul. I therefore welcome our classmates to share some of their memories."

Mary Riley said, "I don't want to brag but I still fit into the earrings I wore in high school."

Bobby Stone told, of the time he fell asleep in English class and started snoring. He said he woke himself up and the whole class was quiet, and then they broke out in laughter.

Jaden Rose said, "You fell asleep in class more than once."

Amelia Martin Ward spoke of the time in second grade when her mother was picking her up and the third-grade teacher Mrs. Peal had on a skirt just like her mom's skirt. Mrs. Peal had her back to Amelia and she ran up to hug her. Mrs. Peal was rightly unexpecting the hug and yelled, "Ah!" Amelia said, "Even at seven years old, I was embarrassed."

Timbo spoke of the time he and Bobby were goofing around in the back of the room in social studies and he passed gas very loudly. He said he blamed a freshman girl behind them. Jaden said, "We knew one of you did it."

Timbo also told of a time everyone remembered when a not-to-be-named teacher came in and lectured with his zipper undone. Another time, the same teacher bent down to pick up an eraser when all was quiet and passed gas.

Mary Riley spoke of the time in seventh grade when she rushed down the stairs to class and tripped and grabbed for nearest thing available. It was George's pants. She said, " George's pants, including his underwear, came down to his knees."

Timbo quipped, "Was that first time you were attracted to George?"

Mary said, "I didn't stay around to check anything out."

"Mary didn't have too much to write home about if she did see anything," George said with a laugh.

Several other classmates yelled out that they remembered that scene but didn't comment further, other than Sister Paula Price, who jokingly said under her breath that the sight caused her to go into the convent.

Dale said, "I remember when I walked down to the donut shop prior to our first class in eleventh grade and got a chocolate chip cookie. I marched around the school with a chocolate chip stuck to my cheek. I didn't even know it was there until we went to gym class during the last hour and I looked in the mirror in the locker room."

Thom grinned. "We just thought you had grown a mole overnight."

Thom commented on how when Dick Vogel's dad passed away, Dick asked him to be a pall bearer. His sister Angie was only four years old, so she told everyone at the wake, "This is my brother's friend. He is going to be a 'polar bear' for my dad's funeral."

Dick said, "Thom and I went to New York City with Irene and Charles. We visited the sites in and around the city. That fall, when their first-grade teacher Mrs. Primary asked what we students had done during the summer, Thom said, 'Dick and I went to New York, and we saw the Spatula of Delivery.'"

"In second grade, Mrs. Collins was going over spelling words and she put the word toad on the board. She said toad, T-O-A-D," George reminisced. "She asked Bobby to spell toad and use it in a sentence. Bobby said, 'Toad, T-O-A-D. I toad Jaden to stop bothering me.'"

Jade added, "I remembered in fourth grade when Jaden brought a dollar to school for a play performance and was playing with the dollar and rubbing it on his face before class. Mrs. Kane, our fourth-grade teacher, told him to stop doing that, as money was filthy from all the people who'd handled it. Jaden said, 'Then if I have a lot of dollars I will be filthy rich.'"

"I remember when Mrs. Kane once created a math problem," Bobby said. "She said there were nine classrooms with 25 pupils in each classroom, how many total pupils were there counting all the classrooms. After some time of working on the problem, Thom raised his hand and said he had the answer—450 pupils. Mrs. Kane asked how he got 450 as an answer. Thom said, '9x25x2=450. 9x25 is 225 students. Each student has two eyes and each eye has a pupil. 9x25x2=450 pupils.' Mrs. Kane just smiled and said, 'I guess I need to be more specific with my math problems.'"

Thom said, "I remember when I came to school without my homework, and I told Mrs. Kane that the dog had eaten my work. I was walking our dog Oscar just before I left for school and had the homework in my folder. It fell out and Oscar grabbed it and chewed it up. Of course, Mrs. Kane didn't believe one of the oldest excuses in the world. She said since I never missed bringing the homework in the past, I could bring it the next day. When my mother had my parent/teacher conference, the subject was brought up and my mother told her my story was really true. Mrs. Kane apologized to me the next day after the meeting."

Jade said, "As you all remember, during our senior year I worked in the office helping Mrs. Murphy perform filing and other duties. Mrs. Murphy answered the phone one day. A freshman's mother was upset because someone stole her son's towel. Mrs. Murphy asked, 'Can you described it?' The mother replied, 'It has the words Holiday Inn on it.'"

Bobby spoke of when he and Thom were walking near the river north of town and a girl about six years old came running up. She said her brother had fallen into the river and he needed help. When they approached the site where boy had fallen in the water, they found that the boy was younger than his sister. The boy went under water just as Thom was about to run to get him. Thom grabbed him out of the water. Once Thom got him to dry land, the boy and girl ran to parts unknown. "We never saw those kids again," Bobby said.

George said, "I remember you guys telling us about that and you two insisted we not tell anyone."

Sister Paula said, "I remember when Mrs. Kane asked me who discovered Pikes Peak as a riddle-type question. I said, I don't know.' She smiled and said, 'I'll give you a hint—it's like who was buried in Grant's tomb. So, who discovered Pikes Peak?' I answered, 'Grant?'"

"I remember when we were all taking drivers training," George remarked. "Mr. Brock was our teacher and you, Pat Hall, our smart aleck classmate, was driving. We approached an intersection, and you were supposed make a right turn. Mr. Brock told you to put your signal on. You said, 'But nobody's coming.' Mr. Brock said, 'Maybe not, but those behind you will need to know what you're about to do.' You turned around and said to Bobby and me, 'I am turning right.'"

Dale remembered, "We had a very active and enthusiastic class. We marched away with first place every year in the float-building competition. What I remember most about the float building was Paul Andriacchi's parents allowing us to build the float every year and supplying pizza for us from their pizza restaurant. We also won the cheering competition each year at homecoming and collected the most money from our Christmas caroling each year for charity."

Paul Andriacchi said, "I remember when we were studying sex education in Mrs. Schuelter's class, and she asked what happens when a young woman reaches puberty. Bobby said, 'She starts carrying a purse.'"

Mollie Clausen laughed and said "That sounds more like Timbo."

"Timbo wasn't attending school at Anytown then," Paul replied. "It was our freshman year."

Mollie said, "I quickly understand those two were like two peas in pod regarding humor in college when I met them both."

Jenifer Ryba played the saxophone in the school band. She was an excellent musician who performed a number of solo presentations over the years, but she needed someone to turn the pages for the music. Carol Turner was her best friend who played the flute. Carol would leave her seat and turn the pages for Jenifer. Soon after Jenifer's first solo, Carol was known by the nickname "Paige" Turner.

Carol raised her hand to be acknowledged.

Timbo said, "Yes, Paige—I mean, Carol?"

After a bit of laughter, Carol proceeded to tell of the time Timbo was in a skit for a pep rally. Students regularly put on skits at these pep rallies. This story was related at the fifth reunion by Emily Townsend, who was a cheerleader. Emily had passed away recently from bone cancer.

Carol who was also one of the cheerleaders, said, "I approached Timbo about dressing up in a bikini for a skit. The cheerleaders agreed he'd be the one to do it. The plot of the skit went this way: Dale was a judge and Paul was a police officer. George was brought before the judge for throwing pebbles into the water, and then Jaden was brought in for the same charge against him. Then Bobby was also brought in for throwing pebbles into the water. Timbo was to come out with the bathing suit on and a skirt covering the bottom portion of the bikini and say, "I'm Pebbles." We explained the skit to Mrs. Richmond, and she okayed it. However, the other gentlemen in the skit talked Timbo into coming out minus the skirt. The skit has been considered a classic over the years. However, Mrs. Richmond and the administration weren't excited about the change in the skit. They indicated no one should try any similar tricks again or there would be penalties."

Dale spoke of the famous sweet roll thievery. "I was always praised for my citizenship. Seniors with good citizenship were assigned as hallway monitors. The job consisted of sitting at a desk to check passes, making certain students didn't lollygag before going to their assigned destinations. This could also be a study period for us, as the monitor didn't have class during this period. There were two other monitors for two other morning periods.

During my period, the custodian would bring three dozen sweet rolls for the faculty. The faculty room was near the monitor's desk. I told Thom and George about the sweet rolls. They didn't have a class during my monitoring period, so I told them whoever received the pass first should cut a sweet roll in half and swipe it so the sweet roll would not be missed. I told them not to come every day. I was the lookout while they were in the faculty room. Somehow the word got out that the sweet rolls were available and the monitors during the other periods were allowing their friends to enter the sweet roll pool. Then one day after a period of time, students were asked to stick out their tongue's prior to going to lunch. The sweet rolls that morning had been laced with food dye and those who'd eaten the rolls were caught red-tongued, so to speak. For some reason, I didn't eat a roll that day, so there were some rumblings that I knew in advance of the trickery. I swear to this day I didn't. My citizenship remained intact."

Timbo said for the record, "We all knew you didn't know about the ambush. Your citizenship was also for honesty with your friends. This was about the only time I ever remember you doing something out of your character. You may have been a thief, but you were an honest thief, if there is such a person."

Dale said, "Okay. Okay, I get it."

No one else shared a story, but probably if they'd thought a little more, they could have come up with number of other stories. The group spent more time individually discussing different memories. Afterward, some individuals adjourned to *Jack's Place*.

*

On December 2, 2002, the gymnasium at Anytown was packed. The occasion was the first varsity boys and girls basketball game of the season. The 1977 Boys State Basketball Champions and the 2001 Girls Basketball Champions were honored during halftime of the girls' game. Buck and John, who had recently been inducted in the MICHIGAN HIGH SCHOOL BASKETBALL COACHING HALL FAME were honored during the halftime of the boys' game. They also honored those players who, during their career, had scored a 1,000 or more points.

Jade Rose, Diana Rose, Nancy Martin Early(Amelia's sister), Carrie Sanborn Jorvarsky, Ben Richmond, Leon Ponzi and Pete Maeder were honored.

Some said they saw someone who looked like Casey Adams in the crowd but weren't sure.

Gerry Martin

ABOUT THE AUTHOR

Gerry Martin Lives in Lawrence Michigan with his wife Judy.
He grew up in a small town near Beal City Michigan.

He and Judy are blessed with three daughters,
two grandchildren, and one great-grandchild .

He enjoys golf reading history and related subjects.

He worked in the health field for 37 years.

This is his second book.

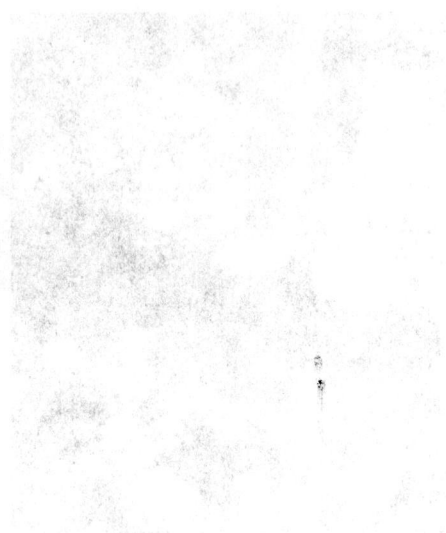

www.ingramcontent.com/pod-product-compliance
Lightning Source LLC
Chambersburg PA
CBHW060016050426
42448CB00012B/2778